SCHAFER'S CASES:
The Hard-to-Find Ones

Schafer's Cases

The Hard-to-Find Ones

By

WILLIAM J. SCHAFER III, A.B., LL.B., J.D.

Assistant Attorney General
State of Arizona
Phoenix, Arizona

THOMAS BOOKS · SYMBOL OF LEADERSHIP

CHARLES C THOMAS • PUBLISHER
Springfield • Illinois • U.S.A.

Published and Distributed Throughout the World by
CHARLES C THOMAS • PUBLISHER
BANNERSTONE HOUSE
301-327 East Lawrence Avenue, Springfield, Illinois, U.S.A.
NATCHEZ PLANTATION HOUSE
735 North Atlantic Boulevard, Fort Lauderdale, Florida, U.S.A.

ISBN 0-398-02399-9
Library of Congress Catalog Number: 79-165898

With THOMAS BOOKS *careful attention is given to all details of manufacturing and design. It is the Publisher's desire to present books that are satisfactory as to their physical qualities and artistic possibilities and appropriate for their particular use.* THOMAS BOOKS *will be true to those laws of quality that assure a good name and good will.*

Printed in the United States of America
Q-1

To my wife, Corynne

PREFACE

Law, seemingly more than most, is a profession of the printed word. Everything we lawyers do revolves around the printed word. Our tools are written opinions; our experience, treatises, case reports, printed court opinions and trial transcripts. We read all the time and yet we do not read enough. No lawyer can keep abreast of the reading material that he should keep up with. There is too much.

The average law office is glutted with weekly advance sheets, textbooks, treatises, law reviews and weekly "quickie" services. The vast majority are never read; most are never scanned and few are remembered. Why? Well one of the reasons, I believe, is that too many words are used. If someone would truly condense what he has to say, more would read it, more would enjoy it and more lawyers would read more.

The few articles and books I have written have been calculated exercises in brevity. It was difficult but by the dint of hard work and shrewd manipulation of a pair of scissors I reduced what I had to say to readable size.

This book is another such exercise. Just enough has been retained to make it interesting, to convey the thought and to make you want to go on. Because of this I am sure you will read more, retain more and want to use this book as a handy reference.

W. J. S.

INTRODUCTION

This book reminds me of a joke that was prevalent when I was a prosecutor in Alaska. It concerned a new judge, quite an intelligent fellow but one who could not make a decision unless he first saw the "answer" in black and white in some legal text. He had to see a "case" before he would allow even the most routine procedures or admit the most admittable evidence. We used to kid the new deputies who were going before him for the first time that they better have a case outlining the state's right to make an opening statement because otherwise the case was subject to dismissal. We never found that case or many of the others that his rulings took us to the books for. We took it for granted that many, perhaps most, points which come up during a trial cannot be answered by looking through a book; they reside with your common sense.

It is true, however, that a great many points which seem to call for simple, common sense answers are not seen that way by others. They, like the judge in Alaska, want something in black and white—a "case." And most of the time such cases are hard to find. Sometimes it is even difficult to know where to look.

So a few years ago I started to collect some of these hard-to-find cases. The book that follows is my collection. It does not purport to answer all the questions, and it certainly does not purport to be a legal treatise on the entire field of criminal law. I am sure, however, that it will provide black and white "answers" (either a holding or simply a discussion) to many of those questions that have stumped you at one time or another—like when you get up to make your opening statement.

The subjects are arranged alphabetically. It seemed simpler that way. Each case is numbered for future quick and easy reference.

CONTENTS

Subject *Page*

SCHAFER'S CASES:
The Hard-to-Find Ones

ACCIDENT

(1) How many times have you wanted to ask an expert what he thought caused the accident? Too many, I'll bet. And how many times have you tried it and been stopped because you didn't have a case allowing it (or even discussing it) at your fingertips? Too many again? After it was all over you probably told yourself that you were going to look it up and see if it could be done. But I'll bet you never did that either. Save your time —I've done it for you. It's all discussed in 38 *A.L.R.2d* 13 (accidents involving autos, trains, factories, machinery, explosions, floods, wind, even "invading gas" are discussed and digested—what opinions may be given and who may give them).

(2) Murder is of the first degree when committed during a robbery even if the killing is purely accidental.—*People v. Riser,* 47 C.2d 566, 305 P.2d 1.

(3) Police coming upon an auto accident where the contents of the cars are thrown about are not required to obtain a search warrant before making an inventory of the contents of the cars.—*People v. Roth,* 68 Cal.Rptr. 49, 261 A.C.A. 466.

ACCOMPLICES

(1) A statute requiring that the testimony of an accomplice "must be corroborated by other evidence which tends to connect the defendant with the commission of the offense" means evidence which taken by itself leads to the *inference* that a crime has been committed and that the defendant is implicated.—*State v. Barick,* 143 Mont. 273, 389 P.2d 170.

(2) The accomplice-corroboration statute is applicable to preliminary hearings.—*Crum v. State,* 383 P.2d 45.

All of this is nothing new to many of us for we've worked with such statutes for years. They are not very complicated but they often are hard to apply to a given set of facts. Just what, for instance, is "corroborating"; when do you have it and how do you know it when you see it? The following cases are examples of some of the usual, and some of the "unusual," places where you might find corroboration.

(3) Proof of the presence of the defendant at or near the time and place of the crime together with evidence of a motive is considered corroborative of an accomplice.—*State v. Sinclair,* 15 Utah 2d 162, 389 P.2d 465.

(4) A defendant's statement that he was worried about the ABC plant and about his name having been called by an accomplice while they were in the plant is sufficient to corroborate the testimony of an accomplice implicating the defendant in the burglary of the ABC plant.—*State v. Barick,* 143 Mont. 273, 389 P.2d 170.

(5) Testimony that the defendant's car was seen at the scene of the crime at about the time of the crime is corroboration.—*Kitchens v. Commonwealth,* 279 Ky. 785, 132 S.W.2d 327.

(6) An accomplice testified that she, the defendant and another man robbed a shop. Evidence that tracks leading away from the shop were those of two men and one woman was corroborative of her testimony.—*Shirlock v. State*, 104 Tex.Cr. 52, 282 S.W. 231.

(7) Evidence that the defendant had burglarized other stores the night of the crime when the defendant set up an alibi as a defense was admissible to corroborate an accomplice's testimony. —*Cochrane v. State*, 125 Tex.Cr. 119, 67 S.W.2d 313.

(8) The state may prove "occurrences" subsequent to the crime charged in corroboration of an accomplice.—*Keith v. State,* 103 Tex.Cr. 636, 282 S.W. 251.

(9) A confession is corroboration.—*Goff v. Commonwealth,* (Ct.App., Ky.), 245 S.W.2d 446.

(10) Corroboration is found in a defendant's signed statement admitting his close association with the accomplices immediately before and after the crime.—*State v. Wederski,* 230 Ore. 57, 368 P.2d 393.

(11) The possession of stolen property is corroboration of an accomplice, even though manual or personal possession is not shown.—*People v. Sanches,* 43 Cal.Rptr. 131, 232 Cal.App.2d 812; *People v. Williams,* 17 Cal.App.2d 122, 61 P.2d 813; *State v. Gates,* 246 Iowa 344, 67 N.W.2d 579; *Wright v. State,* 44 S.W. 151; *State v. Wederski,* 230 Ore. 57, 368 P.2d 393; *State v. Brake,* 99 Ore. 310, 195 Pac. 583; *State v. Broadhurst,* 184 Ore. 178, 196 P.2d 407; *Williams v. State,* 104 Tex.Cr. 55, 282 S.W. 228.

(12) How about this one!

Possession of stolen property is sufficient corroboration of an accomplice even though the property is *not* introduced at the trial and even though there is only a general description of the property showing that the property is of the same kind and evidence that it "is like or resembled" the property stolen.—*People v. Williams,* 17 Cal.App.2d 122, 61 P.2d 813; *State v. Gates,* 246 Iowa 344, 67 N.W.2d 579; *Wright v. State,* 44 S.W. 151.

(13) A film of the crime is *not* sufficient corroboration of an accomplice's testimony where the only foundation for the admission of the film is the accomplice's testimony.—*People v. Bowley,* 59 Cal.2d 855, 31 Cal.Rptr. 471, 382 P.2d 591.

(14) An annotation on the corroboration of an accomplice by objective evidence is found in 96 *A.L.R.2d* 1185 (letters, mortgages, a driver's license, handwriting, a satchel and a sledge, a wallet, movies and photos are all discussed as bits of corroboration).

A few years ago I had a case where one defendant took the stand and started to testify about his involvement as well as the involvement of the codefendant (who was not going to testify). As he started, counsel for the codefendant (the silent one) objected and asked that the court limit the defendant-witness' testimony to only his involvement. That, of course, threw everybody into a tizzie. His argument was that the defendant was an accomplice and as such his testimony was of no value unless it was corroborated. The objection was overruled but only after a long and futile search for a case. Six months later I found the case.

(15) Simply because an accomplice is also on trial (and the state cannot call him to testify) does not mean that if the accomplice chooses to take the stand his testimony is limited to himself. —*People v. Gilbert,* 47 Cal.Rptr. 909, 408 P.2d 365.

(16) I also had one of these a few years ago; I didn't have a case then either.

The occupant of an automobile who encouraged his driver to leave the scene was an accomplice to the crime of failing to stop, render aid and leave identification.—*People v. Holford,* 45 Cal. Rptr. 167, 403 P.2d 423.

(17) This one seems like "one in a million" but one of the men in my office had it come up.

The defendant was tried for burglary; accomplices testified against him and he was acquitted. Then the defendant was tried for perjury arising out of the burglary trial and once again the accomplices testified against him. At the perjury trial these witnesses were not "accomplices" and their testimony did not have to be corroborated.—*People v. Barnes,* 49 Cal.Rptr. 470, 240 Cal.App.2d 428.

(18) An accomplice's testimony may establish the corpus delicti.—*Marr v. State,* 383 S.W.2d 928; *Scott v. State,* 167 Tex.Cr. 77, 318 S.W.2d 650.

(19) The testimony of an accomplice is admissible to prove a conspiracy.—*Price v. State,* 4 Md.App. 701, 244 A.2d 900.

(20) A police officer's testimony concerning the statements made to him by the accomplice was admissible to corroborate the accomplice but it was not competent as substantive evidence of the crime committed.—*State v. Flowers,* 1 N.C.App. 612, 162 S.E.2d 34.

ALCOHOL

(1) An annotation on the admissibility of defendant's refusal to submit to a scientific test for alcohol is found in 87 *A.L.R.2d* 370 (discusses the pros and cons; talks about the theories behind admission and nonadmission; and includes a group of cases discussing the probative value of such a refusal).

(2) Addiction to alcohol is not legal insanity and an alcoholic is held to the same standards of responsibility as anyone else.—*City of Seattle v. Hill,* 435 P.2d 692.

(3) An instruction telling the jury that they may consider the defendant's refusal to take a breathalyzer test is proper on the ground that it authorizes the jury to consider the defendant's silence in response to questions at the time of his arrest.—*People v. Sudduth,* 421 P.2d 401, 55 Cal.Rptr. 393.

(4) A urine specimen is admissible though not taken under medical supervision.—*Davis v. District of Columbia,* 247 A.2d 417.

(5) The defendant is not entitled to counsel when, while in police custody, he is asked if he will submit to a chemical test for alcohol.—*Finley v. Orr,* 69 Cal.Rptr. 137, 262 A.C.A. 711.

(6) Sobriety tests (writing name, picking up coins, touching hand to nose) and motion pictures of a defendant performing them are not in violation of the defendant's self-incrimination privilege.—*City of Piqua v. Hinger,* 238 N.E.2d 766, 15 Ohio St.2d 110.

ALIASES

(1) Evidence of the defendant's use of alias names is admissible. —*State v. Inzerillo,* 191 Kan. 586, 383 P.2d 546; *Fletcher v. State,* 40 Ariz. 388, 12 P.2d 284.

(2) An annotation on the propriety and effect of the use of an alias in instructions to the jury is discussed in 87 *A.L.R.2d* 1217 (a discussion of everything from "alias dictus" to "Martha Laston, alias Martha Washington)."

(3) Once there is proof of the defendant's use of fictitious names, the state is entitled to an instruction that the use of fictitious names may be considered as bearing on guilt.—*State v. Inzerillo,* 191 Kan. 586, 383 P.2d 546.

ALIBI

(1) An annotation on the constitutionality, construction and effect of statutes or rules requiring notice to the prosecution of the defendant's intention to defend on an alibi is found in 30 *A.L.R.2d* 480 (what constitutes compliance, how must the notice be given, may it be oral, what happens if the rule or statue is not complied with).

(2) A statute requiring notice of an alibi before any evidence of alibi may be given is applicable to a defendant who takes the stand to testify in his own behalf. (Meaning, I suppose, that the defendant himself cannot even offer testimony of an alibi when he is on the stand unless he first gave the required notice.)— *State v. Taylor,* 198 Kan. 290, 424 P.2d 612; *State v. Payne,* 149 N.E.2d 583.

(3) What if the defendant files his notice of alibi but then does not present the issue at trial—can you use that failure against him?

The state cannot use against a defendant the fact that he failed to produce an alibi (any evidence of it) after he filed notice to do so.—30 *A.L.R.2d* 480.

(4) This one comes up quite often.

After the admission of an accusatory statement and the defendant's reply which contained a false alibi, the state may introduce evidence, as part of its case in *chief*, to show the falsity of the alibi before the defendant takes the stand.—*People v. McDowell,* 44 Cal.Rptr. 79, 234 Cal.App.2d 54.

APPEAL

(1) As odd as it may seem, this case may well prove handy in the next few years.

The failure of the court to advise a defendant of his statutory right of appeal and stay of execution does not deprive the defendant of any constitutional rights.—*State v. Dodney,* 199 Kan. 449, 429 P.2d 928.

(2) It has been said that a defendant may have a "right" to an appeal but he doesn't have the "right" to a meritorious one.

Although indigent defendants are entitled to court-appointed counsel on appeal, they are not entitled to have the state search until they find one who will contend there was error in the trial. —*Stanmore v. People,* 157 Colo. 207, 401 P.2d 829.

(3) An order adjudging a defendant insane and committing him to the state hospital is appealable.—*People v. Brown,* 399 P.2d 373, 42 Cal.Rptr. 837.

(4) An appellate court did not have jurisdiction to review a criminal case when the notice of appeal was filed *before* a final judgment was entered. (But I'm not quite sure why.)—*Allgood v. State,* 18 Nev. 326, 372 P.2d 466.

(5) When the defendant decides not to stand on his motion for a directed verdict and goes ahead and presents evidence in his defense, a reviewing court will consider *his* evidence as well as that of the state in determining if there was sufficient evidence to support the verdict.—*State v. Camphere,* 233 Ore. 330, 378 P.2d 706.

(6) Where a defendant is convicted and then absents himself from the state past the time for filing his appeal, his absence from the state does not operate to extend the time within which his appeal may be perfected.—*Angel v. State,* 386 P.2d 645.

(7) To reverse, it must appear that upon no hypothesis was there *sufficient substantial evidence* to support the conviction.—*People v. Wilson,* 67 Cal.Rptr. 678, 261 A.C.A. 1.

(8) A reversal on appeal is not a bar to a retrial.—*State v. Bloomer,* 197 Kan. 668, 421 P.2d 58.

(9) "On appeal from the judgment of a district court in a habeas corpus proceeding, it is not the province of this court to review errors claimed, by one of the parties, to have been committed by a magistrate in the course of a preliminary examination."—*Kelly v. Kurtz,* 183 Kan. 684, 331 P.2d 327.

(10) To determine whether the defendant may successfully plead double jeopardy, the trial court may look to the entire record of the former trial and is not restricted to the indictment or information alone.—*Price v. State,* 437 P.2d 330.

(11) An appeal from a decision adverse to the defendant in a habeas corpus proceeding does not suspend the criminal prosecution upon which the defendant is being detained.—*State v. Superior Court,* 56 Wash. 91, 105 Pac. 171, 63 *A.L.R.* 1460, 143 *A.L.R.* 1354.

(12) An appellate court will presume, where the record does not show otherwise, that the trial court explained the defendant's constitutional rights to him before he entered his plea of guilty.—*Nichols v. State,* 418 P.2d 77 (1966).

(13) The test for whether the admission of illegally seized evidence is harmless error is whether that evidence *might have* contributed to the conviction. If it *might have,* it is not harmless.—*Rosenthall v. Henderson,* 389 F.2d 514.

(14) Only the court of appeals may enter an order allowing a defendant to leave the jurisdiction pending his appeal.—*Price v. State,* 396 P.2d 670.

(15) State courts are not bound by federal court interpretations of state statutes.—*In re Elliott,* 446 P.2d 347.

(16) The presumption of innocence disappears upon conviction and is displaced in the appeals court by a presumption of guilt.—*Bartlett v. State,* 429 S.W.2d 131.

(17) This one will probably surprise quite a few groups!

"The Supreme Court is not at liberty to reverse a conviction on the basis of the possibility that the defendant might be innocent."—*Kelley v. People,* 443 P.2d 734.

(18) A trial court will not be reversed for reaching the right result for the wrong reason.—*Rein v. Dvoracek,* 79 N.M. 410, 444 P.2d 595.

(19) "Cases are not authority for propositions not considered." —*In re Tartar,* 52 Cal.2d 250, 339 P.2d 553.

ARGUMENT

(1) Arguments of counsel are not evidence and not admissible as such unless uttered as factual admissions formally made and entered in the course of a trial. The prosecutor's statement at the first trial that "The State cannot honestly say that this defendant aimed that rifle at his wife and pulled the trigger intending to kill her," was not evidence and excludable as mere argument.—*State v. Nichols,* 236 Ore. 521, 388 P.2d 739.

(2) The district attorney's use of the term "burglar alarm" did not entitle the defendant to a reversal of his conviction. (Here the court admonished the jury to consider that the device was only an "alarm" and not a "burglar alarm" and the defendant did not move for a mistrial).—*People v. Hamilton,* 59 Cal.Rptr. 459, 251 Cal.App.2d 506.

(3) A prosecutor's argument that ". . . the conduct of the defendant, including the statements which he has made when he had been informed of the crime that had been committed, may certainly be considered by you . . ."; "you may also consider when this defendant . . . offered an alibi"; and ". . . did he show any shock or disbelief or shock at the testimony of the agent? A big grin, like it was some kind of joke to him" was not improper and not a comment on the defendant's failure to testify.—*Hayes v. United States,* 368 F.2d 814.

(4) Counsel may argue that the evidence against the defendant is uncontroverted and that the defendant failed to produce evidence on some phase of his defense. (This is especially true when the evidence against the defendant could be contradicted by someone other than himself.)—*Ruiz v. United States,* 365 F.2d 103.

(5) The state's argument that both the defendant and his wife committed perjury when they took the stand was not improper.—*People v. Garrison,* 54 Cal.Rptr. 731, 246 Cal.App.2d 346.

(6) The state's argument that "alibi" has a bad connotation meaning the "fix is in" and contrasting the testimony of the alibi witnesses with that of the state's witnesses was not error.—*People v. Garrison,* 54 Cal.Rptr. 731, 246 Cal.App.2d 343.

(7) Where a defendant's witness invokes the "Fifth" and will not testify and the state refuses to grant the witness immunity so that he may testify, the court should instruct both sides that they may not argue a "missing witness."—*Morrison v. United States,* 365 F.2d 521.

(8) It was not error to allow the prosecutor, in argument, to read from a transcript (not in evidence), of the defendant's tape-recorded statement (admitted).—*State v. Cole,* 67 Wash.2d 522, 408 P.2d 387.

(9) Defense counsel was not permitted to argue that the death penalty was not proper in *any* case. The court stated that this argument, in effect, urged the jury to disregard the legislature's determination to the contrary.—*People v. Shipp,* 31 Cal.Rptr. 457, 382 P.2d 577.

(10) The state's argument that even in the face of evidence justifying a conviction, juries sometimes turn a man loose thereby tearing away a part of the jury system which is important to the proper functioning of government was not error.—*Woodard v. People,* 154 Colo. 162, 389 P.2d 411.

(11) The prosecutor's argument, that he "knew that there was no defense to the case and none has been offered so far," was not an improper "comment" on the failure of the defendant to testify. —*Buie v. State,* 368 P.2d 663.

(12) Where the defense was an "alibi" that the defendant was home with his wife, it was reversible error to comment on the failure of the wife to testify.—*State v. Brown,* 14 Utah 2d 324, 383 P.2d 930.

(13) An annotation on the prosecutor's argument that the city, county or state "*wants*" or "*expects*" a conviction is found in 85 *A.L.R.2d* 1132, where you will find such arguments as the following:

"Ladies and gentlemen of the jury, you are being watched by the men and women of this county so they can tell by your verdict your character and the kind of men and women you are in this county."

". . . good men in this county and the best men in Gonzales County" desired the conviction of the defendant.

". . . you black thief, you are a thief, a thief as black as hell itself. Gentlemen, if you don't convict this man you had better throw open the jail doors, tear down our courthouses, and burn up our lawbooks, because if you acquit such men and that is to be the law in Waller County, people will flock to Waller County from north and south Texas to become thieves. All good men in Waller County know this man ought to be convicted, and it is your duty to do so."

". . . the churches demand of you that you do your duty and convict in cases like this . . ." (not reversible).

The annotation winds up with an argument alluding to the "fact" that tens of thousands of poor taxpayers were waiting outside the courtroom for the verdict.

(14) A defense argument that the defendant had a constitutional right to refuse to take a sobriety test is improper.—*People v. Sudduth,* 55 Cal.Rptr. 393, 421 P.2d 401.

(15) A prosecutor's statements that "the defendant was a cold-blooded killer," that the defendant "would like to dance on the victim's grave," and that the "defendant and the codefendant played blackjack or shot craps or played casino while the victim lay in the morgue" were not improper.—*People v. Lopez,* 32 Cal.Rptr. 424, 384 P.2d 16.

(16) Comment by state during its opening statement that the case arose out of a grand jury sitting in secret that was "selected from the same group of people that you were from, sat and heard the government's evidence in the case and then determined that there was probable cause to bring a charge" was improper but did not require reversal.—*Weaver v. United States,* 379 F.2d 799.

(17) Where a "prior" is an essential element of the crime presently charged, it is referred to in the pleading, is read to the jury, must be proved and may be mentioned in argument.—*People v. Shaw,* 46 Cal.Rptr. 217.

(18) Although the state may not express its personal opinion of the defendant's guilt, it may express an opinion based on the evidence.—*People v. Hill,* 98 Ill.App.2d 352, 240 N.E.2d 801.

(19) Argument may refer to a defendant's failure to offer *any* evidence.—*State v. Hampton,* 430 S.W.2d 150.

(20) Where the defense in their opening statement (at the beginning of the trial) promise to prove something and they do not, the prosecution may comment upon such failure in its final argument.—*State v. McGonigle,* 103 Ariz. 267, 440 P.2d 100.

ARREST

(1) Undue delay between the defendant's arrest and appearance before the justice of the peace does not deprive the justice of jurisdiction to bind the defendant over for trial.—*State v. Elledge,* 78 N.M. 157, 429 P.2d 355.

(2) Jurisdiction to try a person exists even though there has been an illegal arrest.—*State v. Cook,* 194 Kan. 495, 399 P.2d 835; *Smith v. State,* 196 Kan. 438, 411 P.2d 663; *Clouse v. State,* 384 P.2d 321.

(3) How about this for ingenuity—or is it myopia!

The fact that the charge was not read to the defendant when he was arrested did not violate his constitutional rights.—*State v. Gibby,* 78 N.M. 414, 432 P.2d 258.

(4) The violation of a statute making it a crime for any officer having custody of a defendant after arrest to deny the defendant's request to communicate with an attorney does not require the dismissal of the charge against the defendant.—*State v. Roderick,* 243 Ore. 105, 412 P.2d 17.

(5) "Presence" in a statute allowing an officer to arrest without a warrant when he has reasonable cause to believe the person has committed a public offense in his presence is to be liberally construed and "neither physical proximity nor sight is essential." —*In re McDonald,* 58 Cal.Rptr. 29, 249 Cal.App.2d 960.

(6) A complaint based upon hearsay may be sufficient to justify the issuance of an arrest warrant even though the source of information is an unidentified informant, so long as the affiant attests to the previous reliability of that informant.—*Hodgdon v. United States,* 365 F.2d 679.

(7) City officers who had a reasonable belief that the defendant possessed narcotics in their jurisdiction and that he might escape unless he was promptly apprehended had authority to arrest and search the defendant where their pursuit of him took them into another jurisdiction (a different city).—*People v. Sandoval,* 54 Cal.Rptr. 123, 65 Cal.2d 303.

(8) In these days of expanding constitutional rights the following case is a handy one to keep in your pocket.

The personal effects of an arrestee may be removed and examined to see if they are stolen. They may be returned to him upon his release or preserved for use as evidence at trial.—*People v. Ross,* 60 Cal.Rptr. 254, 67 Cal.2d 64.

(9) A court has jurisdiction to try a defendant even though he was forcibly brought to the jurisdiction by an officer after an abortive extradition proceeding.—*Call v. State,* 195 Kan. 688, 408 P.2d 668.

(10) "(T)he power of a court to try a person for crime is not impaired by the fact that he had been brought within the court's jurisdiction by reason of a 'forcible abduction.' "—*Frisbie v. Collins,* 342 U.S. 519, 522, 96 L.Ed. 541, 545, 72 S.Ct. 509, 511.

(11) Where an arrest is lawful, the person arrested may not use passive resistance to impede or delay the arrest. A person who goes limp and requires the arresting officer to lift him bodily and carry him in order to make the arrest is "resisting arrest."—*In re Bacon,* 49 Cal.Rptr. 322, 240 Cal.2d 34.

(12) The circumstances authorizing the police to make a temporary detention may be short of that required for probable cause to make an arrest.—*People v. Davis,* 67 Cal.Rptr. 54, 260 A.C.A. 182.

(13) A defendant denied an attorney at the time of his arrest is not deprived of a constitutional right.—*Meyer v. Klinger,* 243 F.Supp. 788.

(14) In an assault with a dangerous weapon prosecution, it is immaterial that when arrested the defendant was originally charged with disorderly conduct and evidence pertaining to such original charge is not admissible in the weapons prosecution.—*State v. Gibbons,* 228 Ore. 238, 364 P.2d 611.

(15) An officer's observations of defendant's drunkenness made when the officer came upon the defendant slumped over the steering wheel in his car which was in a ditch off the highway were admissible though officer had no authority to arrest the defendant for drunk driving without a warrant.—*Puckett v. State,* 363 P.2d 953.

(16) In an emergency situation, police have the right to enter a home even though there is no intent to arrest, search or seize. (Police here learned of a shooting at the defendant's home and entered when his wife opened the door and thereafter inspected the premises.)—*Stevens v. State,* 443 P.2d 600.

(17) Where a statute authorizes a "private person" to make an arrest for a misdemeanor amounting to a breach of peace occurring in his presence, the phrase "private person" when construed in a shoplifting case refers to a stranger to the personal property taken; it does not encompass the owner of the property. So, although a stranger may arrest only when the offense amounts to a breach of the peace in his presence, the owner watching his property being stolen is excepted and may arrest on the spot.—*State v. DeSanti,* 8 Ariz.App. 77, 443 P.2d 439.

(18) The term "presence" in a misdemeanor arrest statute denotes only that the commission of the misdemeanor is perceptible to the officer's senses, visual, auditory or olfactory.—*Jones v. State,* 245 A.2d 897, 5 Md.App. 180; *People v. Sjosten,* 68 Cal.Rptr. 832, 262 A.C.A. 574.

(19) Officers who had heard a police report of a robbery and a description of the culprit were justified in arresting the defendant who fitted the broadcasted description and in taking from him an unlicensed pistol even though it was shown later that the robbery report was false.—*Carter v. United States,* 244 A.2d 483.

(20) Evidence of what information was received on the police radio is admissible in a hearing to determine probable cause for the arrest based at least in part, upon the information broadcasted. (Even though it is, of course, hearsay).—*Hall v. Statey,* 245 A.2d 908, 5 Md.App. 205.

(21) The smell of distinctive odors could constitute evidence of a crime and of probable cause to make an arrest.—*Mullaney v. State,* 246 A.2d 291, 5 Md.App. 248.

(22) Information from official police files and records may be relied upon by the policeman and may be used to establish probable cause for an arrest.—*People v. Sanford,* 71 Cal.Rptr. 790, 265 A.C.A. 1097.

(23) The fact that the only reason the defendant was at the police station when he was identified by the victim was that he was unlawfully arrested did not preclude the admissibility of the victim's station house identification.—*Parks v. State,* 243 A.2d 645, 4 Md.App. 432.

(24) An illegal arrest, search and seizure does not grant one immunity from prosecution.—*People v. Moore,* 446 P.2d 800, 72 Cal.Rptr. 800.

(25) An unlawful arrest cannot be raised by habeas corpus. Once a court obtains jurisdiction, it is immaterial how it obtained it.—*Walker v. State,* 446 P.2d 886.

(26) The crime with which the accused is later charged or convicted is immaterial in determining probable cause to make the arrest.—*Tomolillo v. State,* 245 A.2d 94, 4 Md.App. 711.

(27) The use of deception to gain entrance to make an arrest will not invalidate the arrest as long as no unreasonable force is used.—*Mullaney v. State,* 246 A.2d 291, 5 Md.App. 248.

(28) An arrest is valid although the warrant is not if the arrest was made upon probable cause.—*People v. Chimel,* 67 Cal.Rptr. 421, 68 Cal.2d 436.

(29) The assessment of the reasonableness of an arresting officer's conduct should take into consideration the responsibility of the police to prevent crime and to apprehend criminals along with the fact that they often must act on a quick appraisal of the data before them.—*People v. Mills,* 98 Ill.App.2d 248, 240 N.E.2d 302.

(30) In any probable cause determination the qualifications and function of the person making the arrest are quite relevant and a narcotics officer's actions should be measured against a standard appropriate for narcotics officers under the circumstances.—*State v. Poe,* 445 P.2d 196.

ARSON

(1) There is no requirement in an arson prosecution that every speculative possibility as to the cause of the fire be eliminated. The corpus delicti is proven if the evidence shows beyond a reasonable doubt that the fire is of an incendiary origin.—*People v. Andrews,* 44 Cal.Rptr. 94, 234 Cal.App.2d 69.

ASSAULT

(1) "It would seem beyond any doubt that the jury, as men of ordinary intelligence, could reasonably find, without resorting to expert testimony, that a stubby beer bottle used as a club was capable of causing great bodily harm." (Yes, we might find a consensus on that).—*State v. Anderson,* 242 Ore. 585, 411 P.2d 259.

(2) A flashlight used as a club may be a dangerous weapon.—*State v. Linville,* 127 Ore. 565, 273 Pac. 338.

(3) A statute defining an aggravated assault or battery as an infliction of "grievous bodily injury" is not void for uncertainty—it indicates a legislative intent to describe an injury more serious than a simple battery. (Then why didn't they say that?)—*State v. Blacksten,* 86 Idaho 401, 387 P.2d 467.

(4) "Assault with a deadly weapon" requires no proof of *a specific* intent to commit the offense.—*People v. Claborn,* 224 Cal.App.2d 38, 36 Cal.Rptr. 132.

(5) The general intent required in an "assault with a deadly weapon" prosecution, may be implied from a wrongful act evidencing "wanton, wilful or reckless disregard for human safety."—*Newman v. Larsen,* 225 Cal.App.2d 22, 36 Cal.Rptr. 883.

(6) A good discussion of the elements of the crime of assault with a deadly weapon, how the intent required may be inferred, how criminal negligence fits in, and how an assault with a deadly weapon differs from simple assault is found in *People v. Peak,* 66 Cal.App.2d 894, 153 P.2d 464.

(7) To prove an "assault with a deadly weapon" the state need not prove that the gun was loaded.—*Territory v. Gomez,* 14 Ariz. 139, 125 Pac. 702; *Gonzalez v. State,* 21 Ariz. 385, 188 Pac. 872; *State v. Aldrich,* 75 Ariz. 53, 251 P.2d 653.

(8) A specific intent to kill is not necessary for a conviction of assault with intent to murder; an intent to commit grievous bodily harm is enough.—*Harding v. State,* 5 Md.App. 230, 246 A.2d 302.

BAIL

(1) Only the court of appeals may enter an order allowing a defendant to leave the jurisdiction pending his appeal.—*Price v. State,* 396 P.2d 670.

(2) The charge of a capital offense raises a rebuttable presumption that the proof is evident and the defendant is not entitled to bail until that presumption is overcome.—*Tijerina v. Baker,* 78 N.M. 770, 438 P.2d 514.

BILL OF PARTICULARS

(1) In a bill of particulars, the state should not be forced to disclose its "theory" of the cases.—5*A.L.R.2d* 459.

(2) The people may go to the jury upon any theory within the four corners of the indictment sustainable by the evidence. They are not called upon in advance to submit to the defense the theory upon which they desire to proceed.—*People v. Matthews,* 146 Misc. 423, 261 N.Y.S. 654.

(3) The function of a bill of particulars is not to provide a detailed disclosure of the government's case prior to trial.—*Overton v. United States,* 403 F.2d 444.

BLOOD TEST

(1) Over an objection that it was too remote, the results of a blood test given two hours after the fatal accident were admitted into evidence in an automobile homicide prosecution.—*State v. Cannon,* 17 Utah 2d 105, 404 P.2d 971.

(2) The taking of blood is not necessary to enable a physician to prescribe relief and thus the blood is not "privileged."—*Hanlon v. Woodhouse,* 113 Colo. 504, 160 P.2d 998; *Wolf v. People* 187 P.2d 926; *People v. Downs,* 5 App.Div.2d 935, 172 N.Y.S.2d 377; *Schwartz v. Schneuringer,* 269 Wis. 535, 69 N.W.2d 756. *Contra*: *Alder v. State,* 239 Ind. 68, 154 N.E.2d 716.

(3) An officer's *request* that the defendant submit to a blood alcohol test is not a violation of the defendant's constitutional rights.—*State v. Walker,* 199 Kan. 508, 430 P.2d 246.

(4) The defendant is not entitled to counsel when, while in police custody, he is asked if he will submit to a chemical test for alcohol.—*Finley v. Orr,* 69 Cal.Rptr. 137, 262 A.C.A. 711.

BURGLARY

(1) Proof of the time of the offense of burglary is not part of the corpus delecti. A confession is sufficient proof of the time of the offense.—*State v. Evans,* 45 Hawaii 622, 372 P.2d 365.

(2) A defendant's intent to steal may be inferred from the fact that he broke and entered a building containing things of value. —*State v. Fox,* 159 N.W.2d 492.

(3) Proof that a felony *was* committed after the breaking and entering is admissible to show the intention of the defendant to commit the felony at the time of the breaking and entering.—*Keller v. People,* 153 Cal. 590, 387 P.2d 421.

(4) If the entry is made with the intent to commit two (or more) felonies, there is but one burglary.—*People v. Failla,* 47 Cal.Rptr. 623.

(5) A person who enters a building intending to commit a felony is guilty of burglary even though he had permission to enter either as a member of the public or personally.—*People v. Sears,* 44 Cal.Rptr. 330, 401 P.2d 938.

(6) Evidence that a palm print taken at the scene of the burglary matched the defendant's and that the defendant had never been given permission to enter that office was sufficient to support a conviction of burglary.—*People v. Bright,* 251 A.C.A. 449, 59 Cal.Rptr. 372.

CHAINS OF EVIDENCE

(1) The party offering an object into evidence need not negative a mere *possibility* of tampering.—*People v. Riser*, 47 C.2d 566, 305 P.2d 1.

(2) Demonstrative evidence and its admissibility as affected by the "chain" of evidence, changed conditions, missing links in the chain and the test for admission are all discussed in 21 *A.L.R.2d* 1216.

(3) Items properly mailed to the F.B.I. and returned by them by mail may be admitted into evidence.—*State v. Harris*, 62 Wash.2d 858, 385 P.2d 18.

(4) A "chain" on the murder weapon was rendered unnecessary when the defendant took the stand and identified the gun.—*Washington v. People*, 158 Colo. 115, 405 P.2d 735.

(5) Bottles and their contents were introduced into evidence even though one person who had had custody of the bottles for some time was not called as a witness.—*State v. Anderson*, 242 Ore. 368, 409 P.2d 681.

(6) It is proper for the state to prove that certain physical evidence is not available for trial because it was destroyed after a prior case because the prosecution thought the case was ended.—*State v. Cheek*, 240 Ore. 323, 401 P.2d 27.

(7) Evidence that certain narcotic samples were in a sealed box in a safe in police custody until they were mailed to the prosecu-

tor was sufficient to establish a chain of custody in a prosecution for possession of those narcotics.—*People v. Waller,* 260 A.C.A. 139, 67 Cal.Rptr. 8.

CHECKS

(1) The following case comes in handy when it comes time to argue against a motion for a directed verdict—especially after all you've shown is that the guy passed the check and had an insufficient account or none at all.

An inference of an intent to defraud and knowledge of the fictitiousness of the check is warranted when it is established that a fictitious check has been uttered by the defendant.—*Anderson v. People,* 161 Colo. 541, 423 P.2d 576.

(2) How many times have you needed this one?

In a no-account check prosecution the state need not prove that the check was presented to a bank for payment.—*State v. Kenrath,* 61 Wash.2d 588, 379 P.2d 359.

(3) You better read this one carefully, then check your own statute.

The state may, under an appropriate statute, add together checks issued by the defendant to bring the offense up to a felony.—*In re Dick,* 49 Cal.Rptr. 673, 411 P.2d 561.

(4) An "insufficient funds check" statute does not constitute cruel and unusual punishment. (I'm sure many wives will be sorry to hear this.)—*State v. Nance,* 20 Utah 2d 372, 438 P.2d 542.

(5) Non-negotiable instruments may be the subjects of larceny by check.—*Faulkner v. State,* 445 P.2d 815.

(6) The victim's granting of time to the defendant to pay off the bad check does not insulate the defendant from criminal prosecution.—*State v. Burton,* 444 P.2d 743.

COMPLAINT

(1) Every once in a while the following situation arises. When it does, make sure this case is tacked to your wall.

A filed, unverified complaint is not sufficient to authorize the issuance of a warrant. However, if the warrant is issued, and the defendant submits to the jurisdiction of the magistrate and has a preliminary examination (felony), the defect is waived.—*Harrell v. State,* 395 P.2d 331.

(2) A trial court has no power to dismiss a criminal prosecution over objection of the county attorney on the ground that the complaining witness probably will not testify and that if he did he would not be a forceful witness.—*People v. Dennis,* 433 P.2d 339.

(3) After an indictment is dismissed, the state may proceed on the same matter by complaint and information.—*Stabile v. Justice's Court of Las Vegas Township,* 83 Nev. 393, 432 P.2d 670.

(4) Where several acts can constitute a single crime, an information may charge the crime in one count and the commission of the crime by alternative acts in the same count.—*State v. Scott,* 64 Wash.2d 992, 395 P.2d 377.

(5) A complaining witness has no control over the prosecution of a case and can neither require a prosecution nor dismissal.—*People v. Dennis,* 433 P.2d 339.

(6) An information charging murder also charges all lesser offenses necessarily included in the crime of murder including voluntary and involuntary manslaughter.—*In re McCartney,* 415 P.2d 782, 51 Cal.Rptr. 894.

(7) The dismissal of a charge by a magistrate at a preliminary examination is not res judicata and a second charge may be filed. —*People v. Joseph,* 153 Cal.App.2d 548, 314 P.2d 1004.

(8) In determining whether "probable cause" exists where the evidence is conflicting and different inferences may reasonably be drawn, the conclusion of the magistrate *must* prevail over the conclusion of the trial judge, who saw only the transcripts of the preliminary examination.—*People v. Beasley,* 58 Cal.Rptr. 485, 250 Cal.App.2d 71.

(9) A preliminary examination is not a "trial" and the complaint and warrant used there are not construed with the strictness of papers filed in the trial court.—*State v. Earley,* 192 Kan. 167, 386 P.2d 189.

(10) One count of an information may, by reference, incorporate allegations in another count if the reference is clear and specific.—*Martinez v. People,* 431 P.2d 765.

(11) A charge of assault with intent to commit rape includes the crime of attempt to rape.—*State v. Hall,* 88 Idaho 117, 397 P.2d 261.

(12) A charge of receiving stolen property need not allege the name of the person from whom the defendant received the property.—*Wertheimer v. State,* 201 Ind. 572, 169 N.E. 40, 68 *A.L.R.* 178.

(13) Any person may file a criminal complaint, not just the county attorney.—*Scott v. Justice's Court of Tahoe Township,* 435 P.2d 747.

(14) A defendant may not have the charges against him dismissed simply because he was not brought before a magistrate within a reasonable time after arrest.—*Gottfried v. People,* 158 Colo. 510, 408 P.2d 431.

(15) The dismissal of a complaint in a justice court does not bar a subsequent prosecution in superior court for same offense. —*State v. Weiss,* 438 P.2d 610.

(16) The fact that some wrongdoers are prosecuted and others are not does not, in itself, amount to illegal discrimination.—*People v. Maldonado,* 50 Cal.Rptr. 45, 240 Cal.App.2d 812.

(17) There is nothing unconstitutional in the government having a choice as to what crime it will prosecute when the facts give a choice.—*Minkin v. United States,* 383 F.2d 427.

(18) When a hit-and-run statute is silent as to where the offense must occur, it is not necessary to allege or prove that the offense occurred on a public highway.—*People v. Stansberry,* 51 Cal.Rptr. 403, 242 Cal.App.2d 199.

(19) The short indictment form for murder (A murdered B) permits the state to prove a felony-murder, a premeditated murder, or both.—*State v. Mayberry,* 52 N.J. 413, 245 A.2d 481.

CONFESSIONS

(1) The admission of oral testimony of a confession and then the admission and reading of the written confession is not error.—*State v. Moore,* 61 Wash.2d 165, 377 P.2d 456.

(2) The fact that the accused failed to confess with complete specificity does not render the confession inadmissible if enough is shown to indicate that it refers to the transaction under investigation.—*Rheardon v. State,* 21 Ala.App. 188, 106 So. 510; *Sewell v. State,* 60 Ga.App. 606, 4 S.E.2d 475; *Lancaster v. State,* 54 Ga.App. 249, 187 S.E. 617; *Pretre v. State,* 112 Tex.Cr. 459, 17 S.W.2d 42.

(3) If a confession is reduced to writing and duplicate copies are made by the same mechanical operation, each copy may be considered an original and, therefore, primary evidence and admissible without accounting for the original or the copies.—*State*

v. Trice, 338 Mo. 744, 92 S.W.2d 135; *State v. Lee*, 173 La. 770, 138 So. 662; *Karam & Sons Mercantile Co. v. Serrano*, 51 Ariz. 397, 77 P.2d 447.

(4) However, if it appears that only one copy was signed by the defendant and the state attempts to introduce an unsigned one, the Best Evidence Rule sets in and it will not be admitted unless the state can satisfactorily account for the absence of the original.—*Gordon v. State*, 252 Ala. 492, 41 So.2d 610.

(5) If the confession is reduced to writing and its voluntary character is established, it is admissible as a written confession if it was shown to the defendant or read to or by the defendant and acquiesced in by the defendant as correct even though he did not sign it.—*People v. Shelton*, 388 Ill. 56, 57 N.E.2d 473; *State v. Smith*, 27 N.J. 433, 142 A.2d 890; *Smith v. State*, 77 Okla.Cr. 142, 140 P.2d 237; *State v. Folkes*, 174 Ore. 568, 150 P.2d 17.

(6) Consent to a search is not a "confession."—*Heflia v. State*, 161 Tex.Cr. 41, 274 S.W.2d 681.

(7) A photograph is not an "out-of-court statement."—*United States v. Armone*, 363 F.2d 385; cert. den., 385 U.S. 957.

(8) A confession may not be suppressed prior to trial.—*Wharton's Evid.* Vol. 2, § 350, 12th ed.; 23 *C.J.S.*, p. 271, ftn. 21.

(9) A confession may be reproduced in part through a tape recording and in part through an officer's testimony where the remainder of the tape recording is unintelligible due to some mechanical failure.—*State v. Dills*, 244 Ore. 188, 416 P.2d 651.

(10) The "secret" recording of in-custody questioning of an accused is constitutional and admissible (assuming everything else is proper).—*Lee v. Wilson*, 363 F.2d 824.

(11) Recording a defendant's confession without warning him that it is being recorded does not render the statement inadmissible.—*People v. Lewis*, 53 Cal.Rptr. 108, 244 Cal.App.2d 325.

(12) The testimony of an interrogating officer that "possibly he did overcome his (defendant's) free will" was only a conclusion of the witness and not conclusive on voluntariness.—*State v. Cole,* 67 Wash.2d 522, 408 P.2d 387.

(13) The denial of counsel to a defendant while he was giving a statement was irrelevant where the statement was never used against him because he pleaded guilty.—*State v. Dobney,* 199 Kan. 449, 429 P.2d 928.

(14) The erroneous admission of an inadmissible statement is not grounds for an "acquittal"—a new trial is the proper remedy. —*State v. Phinis,* 199 Kan. 472, 430 P.2d 251.

(15) Inadmissible admissions obtained by a defendant's parole officer cannot be used to impeach the defendant at his trial.—*People v. Barry,* 46 Cal.Rptr. 727, 237 Cal.App.2d 154.

(16) Admissions overheard by a cellmate are admissible if the cellmate acted independent of the police even if the police encouraged the cellmate to learn all he could from the defendant.—*Ibsen v. State,* 422 P.2d 543. See *People v. Paniaqua,* 55 Cal.Rptr. 713.

(17) A cord was found at the scene of a murder knotted in a certain way. The county attorney sent a police officer to the defendant's cell to ask him to tie a knot. He did; it was similar and the state introduced the cell-tied knot at the trial—admissible. The court said there was no invalidating deception and it was not fatal that before the defendant tied the knot, the officer did not inform the defendant he had the right to remain silent and that the officer was there at the request of the county attorney.—*People v. Arguello,* 56 Cal.Rptr. 274, 423 P.2d 202.

(18) The fact that physical or other evidence is taken from one in violation of his constitutional rights will not preclude its admission at the trial of *another.*—*People v. Varnum,* 59 Cal.Rptr. 108, 427 P.2d 772.

(19) A security guard of a county general hospital is not an "authority" who must warn a suspect of his rights before he takes a statement or confession.—*People v. Wright,* 57 Cal.Rptr. 781, 249 Cal.App.2d 692.

(20) The testimony of a single officer that the defendant's statements were free and voluntary is sufficient for their admission.—*People v. Garrow,* 47 Cal.Rptr. 24, 238 Cal.App.2d 424.

(21) Secretly recorded statements of a defendant to a codefendant in jail may be admitted without violating the defendant's constitutional rights.—*People v. Boulad,* 45 Cal.Rptr. 104, 235 Cal.App.2d 118.

(22) A magistrate's statement to the defendant at a preliminary hearing that he may or may not testify but, if he does, anything he says may be used against him did not judicially intimidate the defendant and thus render his statements inadmissible.—*Wright v. State,* 199 Kan. 136, 427 P.2d 611.

(23) It is not necessary that a defendant be informed that the source of his right to remain silent (and his right to appointed counsel if he is indigent) is the constitution.—*State v. Edwards,* 244 Ore. 317, 417 P.2d 766.

(24) By taking the stand and testifying that his written confession was true, the defendant waived any error in admitting the confession.—*State v. Frazier,* 418 P.2d 841. See *State v. Unsworth,* 240 Ore. 453, 402 P.2d 507; *Bell v. People,* 158 Colo. 146, 406 P.2d 681.

(25) Whether a defendant has the capacity to confess is determined by the same standard used to determine whether he had the capacity to commit the crimes. (That seems rather novel these days.)—*Andrews v. Hand,* 190 Kan. 109, 372 P.2d 559.

(26) The effect of mental subnormality upon the voluntariness and admissibility of a confession is noted in 69 *A.L.R.2d* 348 (this note discusses those termed "stupid," "weak-minded," "imbecile," "low mentality," "mentally deficient," "half-witted," "underwitted," "limited to some degree," "a high-grade moron," "dull," "thick headed," and "easily influenced").

(27) The admissibility and voluntariness of a minor's confession are discussed in 87 *A.L.R.2d* 624.

(28) The defense is not entitled to have the jury instructed that compliance with *Miranda* was a prequisite to finding the defendant's statement voluntary. The jury should be told, however, that if the defendant did not understand the *Miranda* warnings they, the jury, should take this into consideration in determining whether the confession was voluntary.—*Coyote v. United States,* 380 F.2d 305.

(29) "Unless a defendant's intoxication amounts to a mania—that is, unless he is so drunk as to be unconscious of the meaning of his words—his intoxication does not render inadmissible his confession of facts tending to incriminate him. The extent of his intoxication when the confession was made, however, is a relevant circumstance bearing upon its credibility, a question exclusively for the jury's determination."—*State v. Logner,* 266 N.C. 238, 145 S.E.2d 867.

(30) Being under the influence of narcotics at the time of confessing (either self-administered or by the police) does not, of itself, render the confession involuntary.—*Bryant v. State,* 229 Md. 531, 185 A.2d 190; *People v. Townsend,* 11 Ill.2d 30, 141 N.E.2d 729.

(31) Statements to an informant on concealed tape are admissible.—*Hurst v. United States,* 370 F.2d 161.

(32) An officer may testify to conversations he heard over a receiver concealed on an informer's person.—*United States v. Jackson,* 390 F.2d 317; *Handsferd v. United States,* 390 F.2d 373.

(33) The fact that before confessing the defendant took a polygraph and the operator told the defendant he thought he was not telling the truth, does not show any inherent coercion requiring the exclusion of the confession.—*People v. Barreto,* 64 Cal.Rptr. 211, 256 Cal.App.2d 392.

(34) A juvenile may intelligently waive his Fifth and Sixth Amendment rights.—*State v. Casey,* 244 Ore. 168, 416 P.2d 665.

(35) A witness does not have to give the specific words spoken by a defendant when retelling the conversation he had with the defendant.—*Lugo v. United States,* 270 F.2d 992.

(36) A good discussion of the famous *Wong Sun* case is found in *State v. Traub,* 151 Conn. 246, 196 A.2d 755.

(37) Motions in limine (which are really pretrial motions to suppress) are discussed in 94 *A.L.R.2d* 1082.

(38) Urging a defendant to "tell the truth" does not render his confession inadmissible.—*People v. Williamson,* 242 N.E.2d 313.

(39) The *Miranda* rules do not apply to a jail-booking officer who asked the defendant his birth date. *People v. Hernandez,* 69 Cal.Rptr. 448, 263 A.C.A. 233.

(40) "It is consonant with good morals and the Constitution to exploit a criminal's ignorance or stupidity in the detectional process."—*State v. McKnight,* 243 A.2d 240, 52 N.J. 35.

(41) The fact that at the time the defendant gave his voluntary statement (and after being warned of his constitutional rights) the only charge pending against him was attempted murder did not preclude the admission of this statement after the charge was changed to kidnapping for purpose of robbery.—*People v. Spaniel,* 69 Cal.Rptr. 202, 262 A.C.A. 987.

(42) "Since appellants retained counsel at trial and on this appeal, they clearly are not indigent and therefore need not have been warned of the right to appoint counsel."—*United States v. Messina,* 388 F.2d 393.

(43) Plainclothes policemen were not required to warn the defendant of her constitutional rights before she smoked a marijuana cigarette in their presence.—*People v. Marinow,* 67 Cal.Rptr. 452, 260 A.C.A. 779.

(44) The statement, "You don't have to advise me of my rights, I know more about them than you. I have been picked up and advised many times before," indicates a valid waiver of the *Miranda* rights.—*State v. Perez,* 182 Neb. 701, 157 N.W.2d 165.

(45) "It should be made clear that once Miranda's mandate was complied with at the threshold of the questioning it was not necessary to repeat the warnings at the beginning of each successive interview. To adopt an automatic second-warning system would be to add a perfunctory ritual to police procedures rather than providing the meaningful set of procedural safeguards envisioned by *Miranda.*"—*People v. Hill,* 39 Ill.2d 125, 233 N.E.2d 367.

(46) Although the defendant confessed the killing of his wife to a friend at a bar and the friend called a sheriff and the defendant then told the sheriff the same thing, the accusatory stage was not reached until the physical facts indicating the crime had been disclosed (discovery of the body back at the defendant's house). *State v. Zachmeier,* 441 P.2d 737.

(47) The testimony of the first officer arriving on the scene of a homicide that, after seeing the body of the deceased, he asked the defendant "who shot him" and the defendant said that he had and who then asked the defendant where the gun was and the defendant went into the bedroom and handed the pistol to him was admissible because the inquiry had not yet focused upon the defendant.—*Longs v. State,* 429 S.W.2d 157.

(48) Under *Miranda,* officers need not warn a person able to afford an attorney that if he is not able to hire an attorney one will be afforded to him.—*State v. Devoe,* 430 S.W.2d 164.

(49) *Massiah* does not apply where, after indictment and appointment of counsel, a third person, without aid from or knowledge of the police, obtains admissions from the accused and then relates them to the police.—*People v. Milani,* 39 Ill.2d 22, 233 N.E.2d 398.

(50) The defendant was not in a *Miranda*-type custody when officers appeared outside his locked front screen door and asked his name, whether he was an exconvict and whether he possessed a forbidden weapon.—*People v. Merchant,* 67 Cal.Rptr. 459, 260 A.C.A. 925.

(51) Upon a guilty plea an involuntary confession is not admissible in a hearing to determine degree of guilt.—*United States ex rel., Sanders v. Maroney,* 397 F.2d 267.

(52) Officers are not required to repeat the *Miranda* warnings every time their interrogation touches upon a separate crime.—*State v. Jennings,* 104 Ariz. 6, 448 P.2d 62.

(53) A plea of guilty is not rendered involuntary by the fact that it was partly induced by the possibility that a more serious charge might be prosecuted.—*Brewer v. Bennett,* 161 N.W.2d 749.

(54) The defendant's self-incrimination privilege is not violated by taking his fingerprints without affording him counsel or warning him of his self-incrimination privilege.—*Washngton v. State,* 434 S.W.2d 138.

(55) Sobriety tests (writing name, picking up coins, touching hand to nose) and motion pictures of the defendant are not in violation of his self-incrimination privilege.—*City of Piqua v. Hinger,* 238 N.E.2d 766, 15 Ohio St.2d 110.

(56) To obtain a valid consent to search, it is not necessary that the officers warn the defendant that any evidence obtained by the search might be admitted in evidence against him.—*State v. Frisby,* 245 A.2d 786.

(57) There can be a valid consent to search even though the accused is not first informed of his right to refuse permission to search, his right to remain silent and his right to appointed counsel. —*People v. Sjosten,* 68 Cal.Rptr. 832, 262 A.C.A. 574.

(58) It is not a search to shine a light upon the defendant's hands to reveal fluorescence which had been picked up by the defendant because he had handled stolen money bags. Also it is not in violation of the defendant's Fifth and Sixth Amendment rights to examine the defendant's hands without first informing him of the reason for the examination.—*United States v. Richardson,* 388 F.2d 842.

(59) Any words which convey the substance of the *Miranda* warnings are sufficient.—*United States v. Vanterpool,* 394 F.2d 697.

CONSPIRACY

(1) An indictment may charge a person with conspiring with other "unknown" persons.—*People v. Roy,* 251 A.C.A. 520, 59 Cal.Rptr. 636.

(2) The conspiratorial agreement may be inferred from the conduct of the defendants in mutually carrying out a common purpose in violation of a criminal statute.—*People v. Cockrell,* 47 Cal.Rptr. 788, 408 P.2d 116.

(3) The prosecution need not file charges against all conspirators. A dismissal against one conspirator does not require a dismissal against any others.—*Bradley v. People,* 157 Colo. 530, 403 P.2d 876.

(4) If a husband and wife conspire together, they cannot claim immunity from prosecution on the basis of their marital status.—*People v. Pierce,* 40 Cal.Rptr. 845, 395 P.2d 893.

(5) Articles taken from co-conspirators after a robbery and after they have separated from the conspirator-defendant are admissible against the defendant at his trial on the robbery.—*State v. Yoshino,* 45 Hawaii 206, 364 P.2d 638.

(6) A conspiracy need not be *charged* to admit declarations of co-conspirators during the conspiracy.—*People v. Lopez,* 32 Cal.Rptr. 424, 384 P.2d 16; *People v. Teal,* 45 Cal.Rptr. 729, 404 P.2d 209.

(7) Where two conspired to rob, a homicide by one while committing the robbery was within the common purpose attributable to both and allowing both to be charged with murder.—*State v. Jensen,* 209 Ore. 239, 296 P.2d 618.

(8) Where two or more people at the same time and place and as part of a common design rape a woman, there is a continuing act of rape and the acts of the codefendant are admissible as part of the *res gestae.*—*Brown v. State,* 435 P.2d 173.

(9) A citizen of the United States may be punished in the United States for conspiring to smuggle amphetamine tablets into the United States even though the acts leading to the crime were committed in Mexico.—*Brulay v. United States,* 383 F.2d 345.

(10) The defendants could be convicted of a conspiracy to commit an abortion even though the intended abortee was not pregnant. (And I'll bet they had trouble with the jury questions on that one!)—*State v. Moretti,* 52 N.J. 182, 244 A.2d 499.

(11) The testimony of an accomplice is admissible to prove a conspiracy.—*Price v. State,* 4 Md.App. 701, 244 A.2d 900.

(12) The mere fact that the actual importation of the narcotics into the United States was done by an undercover narcotics agent did not absolve those initiating and participating in the crime from blame and did not preclude the proof of a corpus delicti of importation.—*Pederson v. United States,* 392 F.2d 41.

CONTEMPT

(1) A note on the power to punish a juvenile for contempt is found in 77 *A.L.R.2d* 1004.

CORONER'S WARRANT

(1) Here's one that will probably surprise you!

A coroner's warrant, after a coroner's jury verdict, takes the place of a complaint and is sufficient authority for holding a preliminary hearing before the magistrate.—*Uhock v. Hand,* 182 Kan. 419, 320 P.2d 794; *State v. Denevan,* 49 S.D. 192, 206 N.W. 927; *State v. Brecount,* 82 Kan. 195, 107 Pac. 763; *State v. Tennison,* 39 Kan. 726, 18 Pac. 948; *Hogg v. Whitham,* 120 Kan. 341, 242 Pac. 1021.

CORPUS DELICTI

(1) It is not necessary to prove the identity of the perpetrator as part of the corpus delicti. Also it is not part of corpus delicti, when two or more are charged with an offense, that there was multiple participation.—*People v. Howk,* 16 Cal.Rptr. 370, 365 P.2d 426.

(2) The discovery of a body or some part thereof is not necessary to establish a corpus delicti in a homicide case.—*State v. Lung,* 423 P.2d 72.

(3) The corpus delicti of first-degree burglary does not require proof of the fact that the act occurred in the nighttime. Proof of an intent to steal or commit some felony, however, is part of the corpus delicti of first-degree burglary.—*State v. Hale,* 45 Hawaii 269, 367 P.2d 81.

(4) "Slight or prima facie proof is all that is necessary" to establish a corpus delicti.—*People v. Hill,* 37 P.2d 849; *State v. Goranson,* 67 Wash.2d 456, 408 P.2d 7.

(5) An accomplice's testimony may establish the corpus delicti. —*Marr v. State,* 383 S.W.2d 928; *Scott v. State,* 167 Tex.Cr. 77, 318 S.W.2d 650.

(6) Records kept by the defendant may be used against him to establish the "corpus" of embezzlement.—*Wigmore,* § 840, 3rd ed.

(7) When the evidence shows illegal possession of a narcotic by *someone* the corpus delicti of the crime of possession is established.—*People v. Bigelow,* 104 C.A.2d 380, 231 P.2d 881.

(8) The degree of a crime is not part of the corpus delicti.—*People v. Bolinski,* 67 Cal.Rptr. 347, 260 A.C.A. 743.

(9) To establish the corpus in a homicide case the state need not eliminate all inferences which tend to show a noncriminal cause of death. All they need do is introduce evidence which creates a reasonable inference that the death could have been caused by a criminal agency. This creates a prima facie corpus and is sufficient even though there are equally plausible noncriminal explanations. In this case there were two possible contrary inferences as to the bathtub death of a 21-month-old child and the court held that a corpus had been established.—*People v. Jacobson,* 46 Cal.Rptr. 515, 405 P.2d 555.

(10) The mere fact that the actual importation of the narcotics into the United States was done by an undercover narcotics agent did not absolve those initiating and participating in the crime from blame and did not preclude the proof of a corpus delicti of importation.—*Pederson v. United States,* 392 F.2d 41.

(11) The corpus delicti of the possession of marijuana may be proved circumstantially by an experienced narcotics officer testifying that the cigarette smoked by the defendant smelled and appeared to be marijuana (even though the narcotic substance is never produced).—*People v. Marinos,* 67 Cal.Rptr. 452, 260 A.C.A. 779.

COUNSEL, RIGHT TO

(1) An appellate court will presume, where the record does not show otherwise, that the trial court explained defendant's constitutional rights to him before the defendant entered his plea of guilty.—*Nichols v. State,* 418 P.2d 77.

(2) A juvenile may intelligently waive his Fifth and Sixth Amendment rights.—*State v. Casey,* 244 Ore. 168, 416 P.2d 665.

(3) The defendant could not object that statements of his roommate were obtained in violation of the roommate's rights where the statements were not used to establish the defendant's guilt but only the reasonable cause for his arrest and consequent search of the premises.—*People v. La Peluso,* 49 Cal.Rptr. 85, 239 C.A.2d 715.

(4) A defendant who was denied an attorney at the time of his arrest was not deprived of a constitutional right.—*Meyer v. Klinger,* 243 F.Supp. 788.

(5) The use of a transmitter and a recording device concealed on a confederate, who had agreed to cooperate in obtaining statements from the defendant did not violate the United States Constitution (4th, 5th or 6th).—*Garrett v. United States,* 382 F.2d 768.

(6) A government informer was called by the defendant to talk. The informer told the government and they said "go ahead." They outfitted the informer with a receiver. The government used a tape recording of the conversation. The appeals court held this proper and not a violation of *Massiah* because not initiated by the government.—*Beatty v. United States,* 377 F.2d 181.

(7) The examination of a defendant by psychiatrists for the prosecuting attorney without the defendant's counsel being present (or any notice being given to him) does not violate the constitutional rights of the defendant.—*Blocker v. State,* 92 Fla. 878, 110 So. 547. Also *Walters v. State,* 22 Ala.App. 644, 119 So. 248 (where court ordered it done); *State v. Myers,* 67 S.E.2d 506.

(8) A defendant may constitutionally waive a preliminary examination without the aid of counsel.—*State v. Crowe,* 190 Kan. 658, 378 P.2d 89.

(9) Defendant's "rights" were not violated by the failure to appoint counsel to represent him prior to his preliminary examination.—*Sanders v. Cox,* 74 N.M. 524, 395 P.2d 353.

(10) A recording of the defendant's statements to an officer after being warned of his right to counsel and to remain silent is admissible.—*People v. Escobedo,* 58 Cal.Rptr. 426, 250 Cal.-App.2d 417.

(11) A defendant's constitutional rights are not violated by refusing to let his counsel be with him during a mental examination.—*United States v. Albright,* 388 F.2d 719.

(12) Where the victim of a crime is working with the police in an effort to identify the culprit from pictures, it is not required that the defense counsel for all those suspected or identified be present with the police and the victim.—*State v. Stamey,* 3 N.C.-App. 200, 164 S.E.2d 547.

(13) The defendant is not entitled to counsel when, while in police custody, he is asked if he will submit to a chemical test for alcohol.—*Finley v. Orr,* 69 Cal.Rptr. 137, 262 A.C.A. 711.

(14) "It is consonant with good morals and the Constitution to exploit a criminal's ignorance or stupidity in the detectional process."—*State v. McKnight,* 52 N.J. 35, 243 A.2d 240.

(15) "Since appellants retained counsel at trial and on this appeal, they clearly are not indigent and therefore need not have been warned of the right to appointed counsel."—*United States v. Messina,* 388 F.2d 393.

(16) Plainclothes policemen are not required to warn the defendant of her constitutional rights before she smokes a marijuana cigarette in their presence.—*People v. Marinow,* 67 Cal.Rptr. 452, 260 A.C.A. 779.

(17) The statement, "You don't have to advise me of my rights, I know more about them than you. I have been picked up and advised many times before," indicates a valid waiver of the *Miranda* rights.—*State v. Perez,* 182 Neb. 701, 157 N.W.2d 165.

(18) "It should be made clear that once Miranda's mandate was complied with at the threshold of the questioning it was not necessary to repeat the warnings at the beginning of each successive interview. To adopt an automatic second-warning system would be to add a perfunctory ritual to police procedures rather than providing the meaningful set of procedural safeguards envisioned by *Miranda.*"—*People v. Hill,* 39 Ill.2d 125, 233 N.E.2d 367.

(19) Although the defendant confessed the killing of his wife to a friend at a bar and the friend called a sheriff and the defendant then told the sheriff the same thing, the accusatory stage was not reached until the physical facts indicating the crime had been disclosed (discovery of the body back at the defendant's house). —*State v. Zachmeier,* 441 P.2d 737.

(20) The testimony of the first officer arriving on the scene of a homicide that, after seeing the body of the deceased, he asked the defendant "who shot him" and the defendant said that he had and who then asked the defendant where the gun was and the defendant went into the bedroom and handed the pistol to him was admissible because the inquiry had not yet focused upon the defendant.—*Longs v. State,* 429 S.W.2d 157.

(21) Under *Miranda,* officers need not warn a person able to afford an attorney that if he is not able to hire an attorney one will be afforded to him.—*State v. Devoe,* 430 S.W.2d 164.

(22) *Massiah* does not apply where, after indictment and appointment of counsel, a third person, without aid from or knowledge of the police, obtains admissions from the accused and then relates them to the police.—*People v. Milani,* 39 Ill.2d 22, 233 N.E.2d 398.

(23) Defendant was not in a *Miranda*-type custody when officers appeared outside his locked front screen door and asked his name, whether he was an exconvict and whether he possessed a forbidden weapon.—*People v. Merchant,* 67 Cal.Rptr. 459, 260 A.C.A. 925.

(24) Officers are not required to repeat the *Miranda* warnings every time their interrogation touches upon a separate crime.—*State v. Jennings,* 104 Ariz. 6, 448 P.2d 62.

(25) The fact that the accused was represented by able counsel at the time of his plea is a fact that argues against his claim that his plea was involuntary.—*State ex rel. Lawrence v. Henderson,* 433 S.W.2d 96.

(26) The fact that the only reason the defendant was at the police station when he was identified by the victim was that he was unlawfully arrested did not preclude the admissibility of the victim's station house identification.—*Parks v. State,* 4 Md.App. 432, 243 A.2d 645.

(27) The defendant's self-incrimination privilege was not violated by taking his fingerprints without affording him counsel or warning him of his self-incrimination privileges.—*Washington v. State,* 434 S.W.2d 138.

(28) The defendant did not have right to court-appointed counsel at a preliminary hearing where he was identified by the victim of the robbery.—*Tyler v. State,* 5 Md.App. 265, 246 A.2d 634.

(29) There can be a valid consent to search even though the accused is not first informed of his right to refuse permission to search, his right to remain silent and his right to appointed counsel.—*People v. Sjosten,* 68 Cal.Rptr. 832, 262 A.C.A. 574.

(30) Any words which convey the substance of the *Miranda* warnings are sufficient.—*United States v. Vanterpool,* 394 F.2d 697.

DEATH

(1) A cause of death may be established by circumstantial evidence.—*Jackson v. State,* 29 Tex.Cr.App. 458, 16 S.W. 247; *Kugadt v. State,* 38 Tex.Cr.App. 681, 44 S.W. 989.

(2) The murder-felony doctrine applies to a case where the victim dies of fright during the course of a robbery (heart attack).—*State v. McKeiver,* 89 N.J.Super. 52, 213 A.2d 320.

DEATH PENALTY

(1) The manner of inflicting a death sentence as cruel or unusual punishment is discussed in 30 *A.L.R.* 1452.

(2) Some good arguments for retention of the death penalty appear in *People v. Love,* 56 Cal.App.2d 720, 366 P.2d 33.

(3) "Nor under the circumstances do we perceive any error in the trial court's refusal to proceed further and hold an evidentiary hearing as to the contention that the death penalty constitutes 'cruel and unusual punishment' or a hearing as to whether the death penalty would interfere with the defendant's right to freedom of religion and speech. Our attention has not been directed to any judicial determination that the death sentence is 'unconstitutional' because it is cruel or unusual punishment, or because it interferes with one's right to freedom of religion or speech. Such being the present state of the law, an evidentiary hearing into these two matters was unnecessary."—*Bell v. People,* 431 P.2d 30.

(4) The prosecution's question to the jurors as to whether any of them had beliefs against capital punishment does not violate any of the defendant's constitutional rights.—*Curtis v. State,* 4 Md.App. 499, 243 A.2d 656.

DEPOSITIONS

(1) The constitutionality of statutes permitting the state to take depositions and use them as evidence in a criminal case is discussed in 90 *A.L.R.* 377.

DISCOVERY

(1) In this case the defense had to produce not only the names and addresses of alibi witnesses to the state but also all written statements or notes of witnesses who testified at the preliminary hearing.—*People v. Lopez,* 32 Cal.Rptr. 424, 384 P.2d 16.

(2) In a rape case where the defendant intended to defend upon the ground of impotency, the trial court ordered the defendant to disclose to the state the names of the witnesses he intended to call and all reports and x-rays he intended to introduce in support of this defense. BUT the court refused to order discovery of the names and addresses of all the doctors who had treated the defendant or the reports of the doctors pertaining to the defendant's physical condition and the x-rays of his injuries.—*Jones v. Superior Court,* 58 Cal.App.2d 56, 372 P.2d 919.

(3) A good collection of authorities on "discovery" appears in *State v. Tune,* 13 N.J. 203, 98 A.2d 881.

(4) A codefendant may discover the statements of another codefendant prior to their trial.—*People v. Aranda,* 47 Cal.Rptr. 353, 407 P.2d 265.

(5) The defendant has no right to discovery and examination of an F.B.I. report in preparing his case.—*Corbett v. People,* 153 Colo. 457, 387 P.2d 409.

(6) Prior to trial the defense is not permitted to discover the written statements of witnesses in the hands of the prosecution.—*Comm'th v. Caplan,* 411 Pa. 563, 192 A.2d 894.

(7) Not even the defendant has a right to see his own confession prior to trial.—*United States v. Murray,* 297 F.2d 812.

(8) The state must produce the written statements of trial witnesses relating to their testimony but the court should first inspect them and excise those portions which have nothing to do with the testimony (but keep the excised portions so the reviewing court can examine them).—*In re Waltreus,* 42 Cal.Rptr. 9, 397 P.2d 1001.

(9) It is proper to deny a defense request to be furnished with a copy of a law enforcement agency confidential investigator's report containing statements of a person identifying a robber.—*State v. Hill,* 193 Kan. 512, 394 P.2d 106.

(10) The function of a bill of particulars is not to provide a detailed disclosure of the government's case prior to trial.—*Overton v. United States,* 403 F.2d 444.

(11) The state is not required to call any particular witness or make any particular test. In an assault case (with a gun) the fact that they did not test the gun for fingerprints or take photos of the bullet holes in the door does not establish any intentional suppression of evidence requiring a reversal.—*People v. Wright,* 66 Cal.Rptr. 95, 258 Cal.App.2d 762.

(12) The state is not required to report to the defendant all they learn about the case and the witnesses (WOW!).—*In re Imbler,* 35 Cal.Rptr. 293, 387 P.2d 6.

(13) Although the state did not introduce the results of a police fingerprint test in a burglary case, this was not "suppression" since all of the elements were present without the can (allegedly used to break into the store) and thus the trial court properly refused to instruct on the suppression of evidence.—*People v. Mestas,* 61 Cal.Rptr. 731, 253 Cal.App.2d 780.

(14) The state's prospective witnesses are under no duty to disclose to defendant's counsel what their testimony will be.—*Corbett v. People,* 153 Colo. 457, 387 P.2d 409.

(15) Because a witness refused to discuss his testimony with defense counsel is no reason to exclude his testimony.—*People v. Spinuzzi,* 149 Colo. 391, 369 P.2d 427.

(16) It is not reversible error to deny a defense request for the production of photographs used in pretrial identification.—*Simmons v. United States,* 390 U.S. 377, 19 L.Ed.2d 1247, 88 S.Ct. 967.

(17) The prosecution is not required to inform the defendant, prior to trial, of the criminal record of the state's witnesses.—*Hemphill v. United States,* 392 F.2d 45.

DISORDERLY CONDUCT

(1) The defendant was rightfully convicted of disturbing the peace when he sang "freedom" songs inside a private business establishment annoying customers and interfering with the business of the establishment.—*People v. Green,* 234 Cal.App.2d 871, 44 Cal.Rptr. 438.

EMBEZZLEMENT

(1) One partner cannot embezzle from another partner.—*In re Sanders,* 23 Ariz. 20, 201 Pac. 93.

(2) In a statutory embezzlement case where a presumption of a wrongful intent is raised by the terms of the statute where an auto is not returned within five days after the expiration of the rental lease, that presumption begins from the date on which the lease expires. (Also, there is an implication here that for the presumption to be applicable, the car must have been driven during the five-day period after the expiration of the lease).—*People v. Starkey,* 44 Cal.Rptr. 738, 234 Cal.App.2d 822.

(3) The records kept by the defendant may be used against him to establish the "corpus" of embezzlement.—*Wigmore,* § 840, 3rd ed.

ENTRAPMENT

(1) A defendant must admit the crime to get an instruction on entrapment.—*Ortiz v. United States,* 358 F.2d 107; *People v. Morgan,* 98 Ill.App.2d 435, 240 N.E.2d 286.

(2) Entrapment can be accomplished only by someone who represents the law.—*People v. Farnum,* 242 Cal.App.2d 310, 51 Cal.Rptr. 327.

(3) A defendant must prove entrapment by a preponderance of the evidence and even though a reasonable doubt has been raised, the burden does not shift to the state.—*People v. Valverde,* 246 Cal.App.2d 318, 54 Cal.Rptr. 528.

(4) Where the defendant and his friends planned a burglary and the police followed them until two of them entered the residence (thus technically completing the crime of burglary), the defendant was not entitled to an instruction on entrapment.—*State v. Murray,* 228 Ore. 567, 395 P.2d 780.

(5) Where the defendant's opening statement stated that his defense was entrapment and that issue was raised on the cross-examination of one of the state's witnesses the state was permitted, in its case in chief, to offer evidence of the defendant's reputation for being a violator of liquor laws (with which he was charged).—*Porter v. United States,* 394 F.2d 508.

EVIDENCE

(1) Evidence that the defendant was "impecunious" (ruinously broke) before the crime and after the crime "flush" is admissible in a trial involving a charge where money has changed hands.—*Sidders v. United States,* 381 F.2d 513.

(2) Evidence that shortly before the robbery the defendant gave his landlady a rent check which bounced and that after the robbery he paid two months rent in cash was admissible.—*Thompson v. United States,* 368 F.2d 318.

(3) The Original Document Rule (sounds auspicious) was not applicable to a "habitual offender" proceeding where the documents were offered to prove the identity of the defendant and they were original records kept by the sheriff of the commitment of persons to his custody.—*State v. Silva,* 78 N.M. 286, 430 P.2d 783.

(4) In an assault with a dangerous weapon it is immaterial that when arrested the defendant was originally charged with disorderly conduct.—*State v. Gibbons,* 228 Ore. 238, 364 P.2d 611.

(5) It is proper for the state to prove that certain physical evidence is not available for the present trial because it was destroyed after a prior trial, in the belief that the litigation was ended.—*State v. Cheek,* 240 Ore. 323, 401 P.2d 27.

(6) The state may show that the defendant was in possession of an instrument with which the killing *may* have been executed (here a butcher knife found in the defendant's clothes drawer). —*State v. Hawkins,* 425 P.2d 390.

(7) In a civil assault case the plaintiff was permitted to introduce a "sap" similar to the one used upon him although the one actually used had a larger handle and was more limber. (Saps, like everything else I guess, just aren't like they used to be.)—*Rich v. Cooper,* 234 Ore. 300, 380 P.2d 613.

(8) The possession of a gun "similar" to that used in a robbery is sufficient corroboration of an accomplice and it need not be introduced at the trial. (Here it was a sawed-off .410 shotgun; but witnesses couldn't say more than that. The only possession shown by the defendant was when he bought a similar shotgun *one* day before the robbery.)—*People v. Henderson,* 34 C.2d 340, 209 P.2d 785.

(9) When the specific type of murder weapon is not known, it may be proper to admit into evidence weapons later found in the defendant's possession if they *could* have been the weapon used.—*People v. Riser,* 47 C.2d 566, 305 P.2d 1.

(10) It was proper in a murder prosecution to show that sometime prior to the murder the defendant had a revolver (make unknown) and it was known that the murder had been committed with a revolver.—*People v. Riser,* 47 C.2d 566, 305 P.2d 1; *State v. Doe,* 146 Mont. 501, 409 P.2d 439.

(11) The fact that an instrument used in a crime is not produced in court does not preclude a witness who saw the instrument from describing it.—*Casias v. People,* 415 P.2d 344.

(12) Testimony of fellow workers that it was general knowledge that the murder victim had a habit of carrying a large amount of money with him was admissible where the victim's body was found without any money on it.—*People v. Roberts,* 246 Cal.-App.2d 715, 55 Cal.Rptr. 62.

(13) An accountant may testify to his findings from an audit of records although the original records are not present in court. (Only photocopies of part of the records were present here.)—*State v. Schrader,* 64 N.M. 100, 324 P.2d 1025.

(14) In a murder prosecution a neighbor's testimony that she heard both male and female voices coming from the victim's house and that the female voice was refusing to give more money to the male was admissible even though the neighbor could not identify the voices as those of the victim and the defendant. (Try that one back in Sandusky!)—*People v. Arguello,* 65 C.2d 768, 56 Cal.Rptr. 274.

(15) Evidence in a burglary case of a footprint in the dust beneath a "new" hole in the ceiling was admissible although it was never identified as the defendant's footprint.—*Battese v. State,* 425 P.2d 606.

(16) The fact that the state had other evidence to identify the defendant's vehicle did not preclude it from showing that the bullet removed from his vehicle was from the gun that had shot at the vehicle when it fled from the scene of the crime.—*Bradley v. People,* 403 P.2d 876.

(17) Officers properly seized in the same receptacle where they found marijuana a letter indicating that the defendant had knowledge of the marijuana and had used some of it. (Now this is too much. I'll bet everybody in the office wanted to take that one to trial.)—*State v. Bunack,* 71 Wash.2d 886, 431 P.2d 195.

(18) Evidence of a diagram of the floor plan of a cleaning plant found in the defendant's apartment when he was arrested for the robbery of a liquor store (not the cleaning plant) was admissible at his trial for that robbery and conspiracy (to rob the liquor store) because it permitted a possible inference of a uniform plan of operation on the part of all defendants. (You won't find many going this far.)—*People v. Collier,* 237 Cal.App.2d 259, 46 Cal.Rptr. 887.

(19) The fact that the defendant *might feel* compelled to take the stand to explain damaging evidence is no reason for excluding such evidence. (But before you do anything further see *Harrison v. United States,* 20 L.Ed.2d 1047, and *State v. Barnett,* 70 Wash.2d 420, 423 P.2d 527.)

(20) The fact that after the defendant struck the decedent he turned to a witness and said "You're next" was material and admissible to establish the defendant's aggressive state of mind when he struck the decedent.—*People v. Ogg,* 258 Cal.App.2d 841, 66 Cal.Rptr. 289.

(21) The fact that the defendant shaved off his beard shortly after the crime *might* infer a consciousness of guilt.—*People v. Slutts,* 259 A.C.A. 949, 66 Cal.Rptr. 862.

(22) A murder victim's letter to mother and her statement to a bank teller that she was going on a trip are admissible to show her intent as to the future.—*People v. Kroeger,* 37 Cal.Rptr. 593, 390 P.2d 369.

(23) Testimony that the murder victim did not allow strangers in her house, that she used her cane as a defense and that she would scream from her bedroom window if she was in trouble was admissible to show the victim's state of mind and also to show that the victim was fearful of strangers and that the murderer was not a stranger.—*People v. Arguello,* 65 C.2d 768, 56 Cal.Rptr. 274.

(24) Articles taken from co-conspirators after a robbery and after they had separated from the conspirator-defendant are admissible against the defendant at his trial on the robbery.—*State v. Yoshino,* 45 Hawaii 206, 364 P.2d 638.

(25) "In a prosecution for receiving stolen goods, the defendant cannot offer in evidence the judgment acquitting the thief as that is *res inter alias acta.*" (I had one of those once—but it broke.)—*State v. Phillips,* 24 Mo. 475; *State v. Ross,* 29 Mo. 32; *Comm'th v. Williams,* 3 Gray (Mass.) 460; *State v. Sweeten,* 75 Mo.App. 27.

(26) On voir dire for determining the competency of a child witness, questions concerning the facts of the crime are immaterial to the question of whether she could remember and truthfully recount.—*People v. McIntyre,* 256 Cal.App.2d 894, 64 Cal.Rptr. 530.

(27) The registration "stub" of the motor vehicle stolen was competent and the best evidence of the ownership of the stolen auto.—*Raullerson v. People,* 159 Colo. 395, 412 P.2d 236.

(28) It is proper to admit hospital records consisting of nurses' notes in an automobile accident case resulting in the subsequent death of a passenger.—*Plank v. Heirigs,* 156 N.W.2d 193.

(29) The admissibility of sound recordings is discussed in 58 *A.L.R.2d* 1024.

(30) The deletion of inaudible, irrelevant or repetitive portions of a tape recording does not render it inadmissible.—*United States v. Maxwell,* 383 F.2d 437.

(31) Although portions of a tape recording are inaudible, the tape is admissible if the import of the conversation is conveyed. —*United States v. Cooper,* 365 F.2d 246.

(32) An authentic and accurate re-recording is admissible after a proper foundation is laid (over an objection that it is not the best evidence).—*United States v. Knohl,* 379 F.2d 427.

(33) An owner may testify to the value of his property.—*Ingersol v. Seattle-First Nat. Bank,* 63 Wash.2d 354, 387 P.2d 538.

(34) The purchase price of an article; its condition at that time; and its saleable value at a secondhand store are elements for a jury to consider in determining the value of an article.—*Lefthand v. State,* 398 P.2d 98.

(35) The prosecutrix in a rape case need not make a direct statement that she was not married to the defendant.—*People v. Harrell,* 252 Cal.App.2d 735, 60 Cal.Rptr. 864.

(36) Hearsay evidence which is admitted without objection may be considered as fully as though admissible in the first place; the only question being the weight to be given to it under the circumstances.—*Eaton v. State,* 404 P.2d 50.

(37) Testimony that the defendant had numerous needle marks on his arm when he was arrested was admissible and material in the defendant's trial for the possession of morphine because it characterized the intent with which it was possessed (morphine is injected).—*Brooks v. State,* 438 P.2d 25.

(38) The state is not required to call any particular witness or make any particular test. In an assault case (with a gun) the fact that they did not test the gun for fingerprints or take photos of the bullet holes in the door does not establish any intentional suppression of evidence requiring a reversal.—*People v. Wright,* 258 Cal.App.2d 762, 66 Cal.Rptr. 95.

(39) Although the state did not introduce the results of a police fingerprint test in a burglary case, this was not "suppression" since all of the elements were present without the can (allegedly used to break into the store) and thus the trial court properly refused to instruct on the suppression of evidence.—*People v. Mestas,* 253 Cal.App.2d 780, 61 Cal.Rptr. 731.

(40) Voice identification is admissible evidence and the defendant may be made to repeat certain words so that the identification may be made without violating his right against self-incrimination.—*State v. Ramirez,* 76 N.M. 72, 412 P.2d 246.

(41) Testimony that the defendant's companion admitted to the witness that heroin found on the ground was hers and not the defendant's is admissible (even if she is not present at the trial and her unavailability has not been established).—*People -. Spriggs,* 36 Cal.Rptr. 841, 389 P.2d 377.

(42) Refusal to admit observations of characteristics or propensities of a defendant during a sodium pentothal test is not error.—*State v. Cypher,* 438 P.2d 904.

(43) The jury may be told that a codefendant has pleaded guilty.—*United States v. Restaino,* 369 F.2d 544. Contra: 48 *A.L.R.2d* 1016.

(44) Where two or more people at the same time and place and as part of a common design rape a woman, there is a continuing act of rape and the acts of the codefendant are admissible as part of the *res gestae.—Brown v. State,* 435 P.2d 173.

(45) Rap sheets from the F.B.I. are pure hearsay.—*State v. Taylor,* 198 Kan. 290, 424 P.2d 612.

(46) If only part of a document is used to refresh a recollection, other parts of the document which are relevant to the part already known to the judge and jury are admissible.—*Gallegos v. People,* 157 Colo. 484, 403 P.2d 864.

(47) The use of memos or writings to refresh a witness' memory does not make that memo admissible.—*Lewis v. Schaffer,* 369 P.2d 639.

(48) At trial a defendant may properly be made to don different costumes, stand up, remove his glasses or reveal tattoo marks on his arms.—*State v. Fisher,* 242 Ore. 419, 410 P.2d 216.

(49) It was proper to permit the state to read and offer into evidence portions of a police report when the defense counsel had previously read portions of the same police report to a witness in the presence of the jury.—*Mabou v. State,* 429 S.W.2d 891.

(50) Where a psychiatrist interviewed the defendant at the request of the state, the psychiatrist was an agent of the state with no more right than any such agent to elicit admissions from the defendant without his being informed of his rights, and his admissions of guilt to the psychiatrist should have been excluded.—*People v. Polk,* 44 Cal.Rptr. 773, 402 P.2d 845.

(51) A case history related by the defendant to a doctor called only for diagnosis and not treatment is not admissible.—65 *A.L.R.* 1217; 175 *A.L.R.* 274.

(52) A physician who has examined a party solely for the purpose of qualifying himself for testimony and not for treatment may not relate the mental history of the defendant as given to him by the defendant.—*Walker v. West Coast Fast Freight, Inc.,* 233 F.2d 939; 51 *A.L.R.2d* 1041; *Reid v. Yellow* Cab Co., 279 Pac. 635 (67 *A.L.R.* 1).

(53) A recording of the defendant's statements to an officer after being warned of his right to counsel and to remain silent is admissible.—*People v. Escobedo,* 250 Cal.App.2d 417, 58 Cal.-Rptr. 426.

(54) Statements to an informant on concealed tape are also admissible.—*Hurst v. United States,* 370 F.2d 161.

(55) On voir dire for determining the competency of a child witness, questions concerning the facts of the crime are immaterial to the question of whether she could remember and truthfully recount.—*People v. McIntyre,* 256 Cal.App.2d 894, 64 Cal.Rptr. 530.

(56) The removal of a particle of fabric from the exterior of the fender of the defendant's car parked outside the courthouse was not in violation of the Fourth Amendment.—*Smith v. Commonwealth,* 424 S.W.2d 835.

(57) The affidavit for a search warrant may be supplemented by the magistrate's personal interrogation of the affiant.—*State v. Campbell,* 161 N.W.2d 47.

(58) "Probable cause" for a search may rest upon evidence which would not be competent at a trial.—*State v. Kasabucki,* 52 N.J. 110, 244 A.2d 101.

(59) The testimony of codefendants may be considered as to defendant's guilt.—*People v. Lynam,* 261 A.C.A. 560, 68 Cal.Rptr. 202.

(60) The state is permitted to take the fingerprints of the defendant in the courtroom during the trial.—*United States v. Rundle,* 384 F.2d 997

(61) An officer could refresh his recollection from an unsigned statement of the defendant whose questions and answers the officer had typed.—*Miller v. State,* 251 Md. 362, 247 A.2d 530.

(62) The fact that a witness failed to identify another person involved in the robbery has no bearing or materiality to the witness' identification of the defendant.—*State v. Hunsucker,* 3 N.C.App. 281, 164 S.E.2d 507.

(63) A urine specimen is admissible although not taken under medical supervision.—*Davis v. District of Columbia,* 247 A.2d 417.

(64) A physician may testify to the results of a test even though he did not personally conduct the test and was not personally familiar with the procedures of the test but was responsible for the results of the test.—*State v. Salter,* 162 N.W.2d 427.

(65) Hearsay may be used in establishing probable cause to search and seize.—*People v. Hale,* 262 A.C.A. 876, 69 Cal.Rptr. 28.

(66) Excluded evidence under the Fourth Amendment may be introduced for impeachment purposes.—*State v. Cannito,* 183 Neb. 575, 162 N.W.2d 260.

(67) A victim's declarations are not inadmissible at the trial even though the victim himself was ruled incompetent as a witness.—*State v. Simmons,* 52 N.J. 538, 247 A.2d 313.

(68) Testimony that the house where the killing occurred was in Ware County was not a "mere conclusion" and was admissible. —*Holmes v. State,* 224 Ga. 553, 163 S.E.2d 803.

(69) Where there was an issue as to the amount of money stolen it was not in violation of the Best Evidence Rule to permit oral testimony by the victim as to how much was taken although he also testified that he had made calculations on an adding machine.—*State v. Swanson,* 440 P.2d 492.

(70) Permitting federal agents to testify that the records of the Department of the Interior showed no application of the defendant for permission to possess more than the statutory limit of mourning doves was not error as against an objection based upon the Best Evidence Rule. *Aiuppa v. United States,* 393 F.2d 597.

(71) The jury may disbelieve the testimony of a psychiatrist.—*People v. Scott,* 11 McA. 576, 161 N.W.2d 753.

EXCULPATORY STATEMENTS

(1) Statements by an accomplice, when stopped with the defendant, that the beer, metal tent stake and bolt (all products of a burglary) found in the car were his were not admissible as admissions because they were exculpatory (he explained away their presence).—*State v. Garrison,* 71 Wash.2d 312, 427 P.2d 1012.

(2) The state is bound by exculpatory statements in a confession unless the evidence shows them to be untrue (and this may be done by circumstantial, as well as direct evidence).—*Dean v. State,* 381 P.2d 178.

EXHIBITS

(1) As to court exhibits, the better practice is to remove the police identification tags before admission.—*State v. Velasquez,* 67 Wash.2d 138, 406 P.2d 772.

(2) Photos of the victim upon which the witness had circled with red areas described in his testimony were admissible.—*State v. Hedin,* 67 Wash.2d 542, 408 P.2d 245.

(3) An objection to the admission of an exhibit is waived if the party objecting thereafter uses the exhibit for his own purposes.—*Sevener v. Northwest Tractor & Equipment Corp.,* 41 Wash.2d 1, 247 P.2d 237; *State v. Scott,* 237 Ore. 390, 390 P.2d 328.

(4) The test for the admission of an object for *illustrative purposes* is that it be relevant and material and that it be substantially like the real object in function and operation.—*State v. Gray,* 64 Wash.2d 979, 395 P.2d 490.

(5) Although a witness misstated the serial number of the murder weapon this did not render the identification inadequate and the gun was admissible where the witness said it was the one he sold to the defendant. The mistated serial number went to credibility, not admissibility.—*State v. Jackson,* 235 Ore. 481, 385 P.2d 623.

(6) The test for the admission of an object is whether it is reasonably certain that there was no alteration of it.—*Dobson v. Ind. Acc. Comm'n,* 251 P.2d 349.

(7) A proper foundation for the admissibility of a drawing does not require the drawer to testify.—*Pedersen v. State,* 420 P.2d 327.

(8) It is not necessary that the object offered in evidence be in precisely the same condition as when it was used.—*State v. Olsen,* 241 Ore. 212, 405 P.2d 358.

EXPERTS

(1) An expert may express his opinion in terms of "possibility," "probability" or "actuality."—*Lester v. State,* 416 P.2d 52.

(2) An expert's testimony that hair samples were *probably* from the decedent did not render his testimony inadmissible.—*State v. Harris,* 241 Ore. 224, 405 P.2d 492.

(3) An expert may testify to the facts upon which he bases his opinion even though they come from sources which themselves are inadmissible or inaccurate.—*Dept. of Public Works v. DiTomasco,* 57 Cal.Rptr. 293, 248 Cal.App.2d 741.

(4) An expert's testimony is admissible even though his testimony relates to a small quantity of material that was consumed in a chemical analysis to determine its composition.—*Casias v. People,* 415 P.2d 344.

(5) A medical expert may testify to matters of expertness although he is not licensed to practice medicine in the jurisdiction where he is testifying.—*Hayes v. United States,* 367 F.2d 216.

(6) An expert may give an opinion as to whether narcotics were possessed for sale by the defendant (after testifying as to his experience with the habits of users, quantities involved. the value of the narcotics found in defendant's possession and the customary method of packaging narcotics for use and sale).—*People v. Arguello,* 53 Cal.Rptr. 245, 244 Cal.App.2d 413.

(7) A director of a safety council who had been a sheriff for fourteen years and whose avocation was guns for thirty years could testify that the fatal arm wound could not have been inflicted by a bullet from the decedent's gun at close range.—*State v. Nelson,* 432 P.2d 857.

(8) A nonexpert investigating officer who had already testified to the skid marks found at the point of impact, the apparent automobile direction, and the damage is permitted to indicate the position of the automobiles as they collided even though this is an opinion.—*Duran v. Mueller,* 79 Nev. 453, 386 P.2d 733.

(9) A witness other than a physician may, by training, study, and experience, or special familiarity with the subject, be qualified to testify as to the cause of death (in the discretion of the court). Here a licensed embalmer, funeral director and special investigator gave his opinion on cause of death.)—*Harvell v. State,* 395 P.2d 331.

(10) A physician's testimony as to the results of a blood test is admissible although he himself did not perform the blood test (his assistant did).—*State v. Boehme,* 71 Wash.2d 621, 430 P.2d 527.

(11) An autopsy surgeon was permitted to testify to the murder victim's ability to talk after he had been wounded, and the victim's perceptive powers after being wounded, even though the surgeon had never treated a person for a bullet wound.—*People v. Ketchel,* 30 Cal.Rptr. 538, 381 P.2d 394.

(12) A doctor, in arriving at his opinion on insanity, may use materials gathered from psychological tests given by psychologists under his direction.—*State v. Coltharp,* 199 Kan. 598, 433 P.2d 418.

(13) Allowing the pathologist who performed the autopsy on the victim of a vehicular manslaughter to answer a hypothetical question on the cause of the injuries was not error.—*State v. Wade,* 159 N.W.2d 396.

(14) Expert testimony that motion picture films showing the defendant beating a person were not retouched, showed no use of cosmetics and accurately represented the scene before the camera, sufficiently authenticated the films to render them admissible.—*People v. Samuels,* 58 Cal.Rptr. 439, 250 Cal.App.2d 501.

(15) A lay witness who is sufficiently trained and experienced can testify to the reaction of users of drugs. Here the lay witness who was permitted to testify to this was an officer with two years on the narcotics squad, who had played the role of an addict while associating with users, who had special training in the use and methods of administering narcotics, who had been taught to observe users and their reactions and who had observed twenty to thirty people under the influence of heroin and withdrawing from it.—*State v. Chavez,* 77 N.M. 274, 421 P.2d 796.

(16) Testimony of an officer that the defendant had numerous needle marks on his arm when arrested was admissible and material at the defendant's trial for the possession of morphine because it characterized the intent with which it was possessed (morphine is injected).—*Brooks v. State,* 438 P.2d 25.

(17) A police officer was allowed to testify as to whether the lack of visible scars on someone's arms would indicate whether he had been using heroin by way of intravenous injection.—*People v. Cruz,* 66 Cal.Rptr. 772, 260 A.C.A. 55.

(18) A police officer was permitted to identify that a one-inch "roach" found on the floorboard of an automobile was marijuana. —*People v. Perez,* 66 Cal.Rptr. 473, 259 A.C.A. 391.

(19) The corpus delicti of the possession of marijuana may be proved circumstantially by an experienced narcotics officer testifying that the cigarette smoked by the defendant smelled and appeared to be marijuana (and the narcotic substance was never produced).—*People v. Marinos,* 67 Cal.Rptr. 452, 260 A.C.A. 779.

(20) The jury may disbelieve the testimony of a phychiatrist.—*People v. Scott,* 11 McA. 576, 161 N.W.2d 753.

FALSE PRETENSES

(1) The fact that the victims were careless because they did not first read the document handed to them before signing it was no defense to a charge of theft by false pretenses.—*People v. Breslin,* 245 Cal.App.2d 232, 53 Cal.Rptr. 687.

FELONY

(1) A peace officer may arrest without a warrant when the defendant has committed a felony and "felony" includes a crime, like indecent exposure, which is only a felony because the defendant has a prior conviction for indecent exposure.—*People v. Succop,* 57 Cal.Rptr. 269.

(2) Where a prior conviction (charged) makes the offense a felony, the offense charged does not become a misdemeanor when the prior conviction is admitted and the defendant is still subject to imprisonment as a felon and the offense is cognizable in superior court.—*People v. Shaw,* 46 Cal.Rptr. 217.

(3) Where the defendant was given probation on the condition that he spend the first ten months in the county jail, the condition did not render the crime a misdemeanor.—*People v. Esparza,* 61 Cal.Rptr. 167, 253 Cal.App.2d 362.

FLIGHT

(1) "Flight" consisted of a trip from the bedroom to the kitchen when officers entered with a search warrant in a prosecution for possession of heroin for sale and possession of marijuana.—*People v. Zavala,* 239 Cal.App.2d 732, 49 Cal.Rptr. 129.

(2) An instruction on flight was proper even though the defendant did not fly until a week after the crime.—*State v. Bryant,* 437 P.2 398.

FORGERY

(1) The signing of a credit charge or sales slip as forgery is discussed in 90 *A.L.R.2d* 822.

(2) To prove "attempting to pass a forged check," it is not necessary that the check be endorsed.—*Dickerson v. State,* 124 P.2d 750; *People v. Van Baron,* 295 Pac. 68.

(3) A defendant's knowledge that an instrument was forged may be found by the jury's conclusion that the defendant had *reason to believe* it was forged.—*Hurley v. State,* 416 P.2d 967.

(4) A misspelling of the drawer's name on a forged check is not fatal to the prosecution.—*State v. Cooper,* 146 Mont. 336, 406 P.2d 691.

HABEAS CORPUS

(1) A discharge upon habeas corpus for failure of proof (lack of probable cause) does not bar further prosecution upon another indictment for the same offense.—*In re Begerow,* 136 Cal. 393, 68 Pac. 773.

(2) An appeal from a decision adverse to the defendant in a habeas corpus action does not suspend the criminal prosecution which is the basis for the defendant's detention.—*State v. Superior Court,* 105 Pac. 171, 63 *A.L.R.* 1460, 143 *A.L.R.* 1854.

(3) Habeas corpus is not available to determine if at the time the defendant entered his plea he was insane.—*Reid v. Raines,* 368 P.2d 668.

(4) In habeas corpus, prohibition or certiorari proceedings, "jurisdiction" is not limited to its fundamental meaning, and judicial acts may be restrained or annulled if it is determined that they are in excess of a court's powers as defined by the constitution, a statute, or court rules.—*In re Zerbe,* 36 Cal.Rptr. 286, 388 P.2d 182.

(5) If a defendant desires a speedy trial he should move for it by way of a *habeas corpus ad prosequendum.*—*Gunter v. Okla. County Dist. Ct.,* 434 P.2d 493.

(6) An unlawful arrest cannot be raised by habeas corpus. Once a court obtains jurisdiction it is immaterial how it obtained it.—*Walker v. State,* 92 Idaho 517, 446 P.2d 886.

HANDWRITING

(1) Where exemplars and the questioned writing are in evidence a comparison may be made by the jury with or without the aid of the handwriting expert's testimony and the results of the comparisons are a matter for the jury.—*People v. Weiskopf,* 60 Cal.App.2d 214, 140 P.2d 201; *People v. Horowitz,* 70 Cal.App.2d 675, 161 P.2d 833, 80 *A.L.R.2d* 272, 275, 276, 277.

(2) Anyone who is familiar with a person's handwriting from having seen him write is competent as a nonexpert witness to give his opinion on the genuineness of such person's signature.—*State v. Eubanks,* 86 Idaho 32, 383 P.2d 342.

HEARSAY

(1) Testimony that a telephone conversation took place is not objectionable as hearsay.—*People v. Gonzales,* 67 Cal.Rptr. 551, 439 P.d 655.

(2) What the owner said to a police officer when she discovered the theft of her auto was admissible as a spontaneous utterance in the trial for the theft of the auto.—*State v. Crawley,* 242 Ore. 601, 410 P.2d 1012.

(3) An officer's recounting of a bystander's description of the getaway automobile is admissible as a spontaneous declaration.—*People v. Cooper,* 64 Cal.Rptr. 282, 256 Cal.App.2d 500.

(4) The murder victim's letter to her mother and a statement to a bank teller that she was going on a trip are admissible to show her intent as to the future.—*People v. Kroeger,* 37 Cal.Rptr. 593, 390 P.2d 369.

(5) Testimony that the murder victim did not allow strangers in her house, that she used her cane as a defense and that she would scream from her bedroom window if she was in trouble was admissible to show the victim's state of mind and also to show that the victim was fearful of strangers and that the murderer was not a stranger.—*People v. Arguello,* 56 Cal.Rptr. 274, 65 Cal.2d 768.

(6) An officer may testify to conversations he heard over a receiver concealed on an informer's person.—*United States v. Jackson,* 390 F.2d 317; *Handsferd v. United States,* 390 F.2d 373.

(7) An officer's testimony that the defendant's companion admitted to him that the heroin found on the ground was hers and not his is admissible as an admission against interest (hers) (even if she is not present at the trial and her unavailability has not been established).—*People v. Spriggs,* 36 Cal.Rptr. 841, 389 P.2d 377.

(8) A neighbor testified in the murder trial that she heard male and female voices coming from the dead widow's house and a female voice refusing to give more money. This was not hearsay when offered to prove that the man to whom the victim spoke believed she would not give him any more money because this was a matter bearing on the question of motive. Also it was hearsay when it was offered to prove the widow's state of mind or intent not to loan any more money but admissible under the exception relating to the mental state of the declarant.—*People v. Arguello,* 56 Cal.Rptr. 274, 65 Cal.2d 768.

(9) Statements of a third person in answer to inquiries about an absent witness and the inquiries themselves are admissible to prove that a diligent search for the witness was made.—*People v. Thomas,* 164 Cal.App.2d 571, 331 P.2d 82.

(10) Hearsay evidence which is admitted without objection may be considered as fully as though admissible in the first place; the only question being the weight which should be given to it under circumstances.—*Eaton v. State,* 404 P.2d 50.

(11) The registration "stub" of the motor vehicle stolen was competent and the best evidence of the ownership of the stolen auto.—*Raullerson v. People,* 159 Colo. 395, 412 P.2d 236.

(12) It is proper to admit hospital records consisting of nurses' notes in an automobile accident case resulting in the subsequent death of a passenger.—*Plank v. Heirigs*, 156 N.W.2d 193.

(13) The testimony of a third person who heard or observed an extrajudicial identification is admissible as an exception to the hearsay rule.—*People v. Pedercine*, 63 Cal.Rptr. 873; *Gallegos v. People*, 157 Colo. 484, 403 P.2d 864.

(14) Rap sheets from the F.B.I. are pure hearsay.—*State v. Taylor*, 198 Kan. 290, 424 P.2d 612.

(15) Where two or more people at the same time and place and as part of a common design rape a woman, there is a continuing act of rape and the acts of the codefendant are admissible as part of the *res gestae*.—*Brown v. State*, 435 P.2d 173.

(16) The testimony of codefendants may be considered as to defendant's guilt.—*People v. Lynam*, 68 Cal.Rptr. 202, 261 A.C.A. 560.

(17) A police officer's testimony concerning the statements made to him by an accomplice of the defendant was admissible to corroborate the testimony of the accomplice but it was not competent as substantive evidence of the crime committed.—*State v. Flowers*, 1 N.C.App. 612, 162 S.E.2d 34.

(18) Evidence of what information was received on the police radio is admissible in a hearing to determine probable cause (even though hearsay).—*Hall v. Statev*, 5 Md.App. 205, 245 A.2d 908.

(19) Information from official police files and records may be relied upon by the policemen and may be used to establish probable cause for an arrest.—*People v. Sanford*, 71 Cal.Rptr. 790, 265 A.C.A. 1097.

(20) A physician may testify to the results of a test even though he did not personally conduct the test and was not personally familiar with the procedures of the test but was responsible for the results of the test.—*State v. Salter,* 162 N.W.2d 427.

(21) A vicim's declarations were not inadmissible at the trial even though the victim himself was ruled incompetent as a witness.—*State v. Simmons,* 52 N.J. 538, 247 A.2d 313.

(22) Where there was an issue as to the amount of money stolen it was not in violation of the Best Evidence Rule to permit oral testimony by the victim as to how much was taken although he also testified that he had made calculations on an adding machine.—*State v. Swanson,* 440 P.2d 492.

(23) Permitting federal agents to testify that the records of the Department of the Interior showed no application of the defendant for permission to possess more than the statutory limit of mourning doves was not error as against an objection based upon the Best Evidence Rule.—*Aiuppa v. United States,* 393 F.2d 597.

HOMICIDE

(1) To show a corpus delicti of murder the state need not produce the dead body or evidence of the means used to produce death.—*People v. Bolinski,* 67 Cal.Rptr. 347, 260 A.C.A. 347.

(2) Circumstantial evidence is as good in a homicide case as in any other case.—*Drake v. State,* 437 P.2d 461.

(3) A discussion of death from assaults where the defendant used only his fists or feet is found in 22 *A.L.R.2d* 846.

(4) "To establish a corpus in a homicide case the state need not eliminate all inferences which tend to show a non-criminal cause of death. All they need do is introduce evidence which creates a reasonable inference that the death could have been caused by a criminal agency. This creates a prima facie corpus and is sufficient even though there are equally plausible non-criminal explanations of the event." (In this case there were two possible contrary inferences as to the bathtub death of a 21-month-old child and the court held that a corpus had been established).—*People v. Jacobson,* 46 Cal.Rptr. 515, 405 P.2d 555.

(5) A statute, providing that "on proof of the killing the burden of proving circumstances of mitigation, justification or excuse devolves upon the accused unless the state's proof sufficiently manifests that the crime amounted only to manslaughter or that accused was justified or excused in committing homicide" is not invalid because it places on the defendant the burden of proving his innocence. Such a statute merely places on him the burden of raising a reasonable doubt as to his guilt.—*Leonard v. People,* 149 Colo. 360, 369 P.2d 54; *Jackson v. Superior Court,* 42 Cal.-Rptr. 838, 399 P.2d 374.

(6) If the murder takes place while the defendant is carrying a firearm in violation of a statute which prohibits convicted felons from carrying firearms, the murder-felony rule applies and it is murder in the second degree.—*People v. Schader,* 44 Cal.-Rptr. 193, 401 P.2d 665.

(7) A homicide which is a direct and causal result of the commission of a felony inherently dangerous to human life, if other than the felonies enumerated in the murder-felony statute, is second-degree murder.—*People v. Ford,* 36 Cal.Rptr. 620, 388 P.2d 892.

(8) One who voluntarily drinks himself into unconsciousness intends whatever the foreseeable consequences or inevitable results of such intoxication are, and that intent may be sufficient for second-degree murder.—*Watkins v. People,* 158 Colo. 485, 408 P.2d 425.

(9) The necessity that the court charge upon motive in a homicide case is discussed in 71 *A.L.R.2d* 1025.

(10) Murder by auto is discussed in 21 *A.L.R.3rd* 116.

(11) First-degree murder requires express malice; murder second consists of implied malice.—*Ingles v. People,* 92 Colo. 518, 22 P.2d 1109.

(12) Although one who commits euthanasia bears no ill will toward his victim and believes his act is morally justified, he nevertheless legally acts with malice if he is able to comprehend that society prohibits his act regardless of his belief.—*People v. Conley,* 49 Cal.Rptr. 815, 411 P.2d 911.

(13) An actual intent to kill is not necessary for second-degree murder.—*Jackson v. Superior Court,* 42 Cal.Rptr. 838, 399 P.2d 374.

(14) Where two conspired to rob, a homicide by one while committing the robbery is within the common purpose and attributable to both.—*State v. Jensen,* 209 Ore. 239, 296 P.2d 618.

(15) The discovery of a body or some part thereof is not necessary to establish the corpus delicti in a homicide case.—*State v. Lung,* 70 Wash.2d 365, 423 P.2d 72.

(16) A cause of death may be established by circumstantial evidence.—*Jackson v. State,* 16 S.W. 247; *Kugadt v. State,* 44 S.W. 989.

(17) A specific intent to kill is not necessary for a conviction of assault with intent to murder; an intent to commit grievous bodily harm is enough.—*Harding v. State,* 246 A.2d 302.

(18) A defendant may be convicted of a felony-murder even though, at the time of the trial, the felony has been barred by the statute of limitations.—*People v. Lilliock,* 71 Cal.Rptr. 434, 265 A.C.A. 434.

(19) The short indictment form for murder (A murdered B) permitted the state to prove a felony-murder, a premeditated murder, or both.—*State v. Mayberry,* 52 N.J. 413, 245 A.2d 481.

IDENTIFICATION

(1) The degree of positiveness in identification goes only to the weight of such testimony; not its admissibility.—*People v. Gonzales,* 67 Cal.Rptr. 551, 439 P.2d 665; *People v. Spinuzzi,* 149 Colo. 391, 369 P.2d 427 (where the witness said, "I am not sure but I think I recognize him"—admissible).

(2) There is no requirement that mug shots seen by victim in identifying the defendant be produced by the state as part if its foundation for the witness' in-court identification. (But beware —this case is before *Wade & Stovall*).—*People v. Bryant,* 64 Cal.-Rptr. 86, 256 Cal.App.2d 470.

(3) The admissibility of extrajudicial or pretrial identifications is found in 71 *A.L.R.2d* 449.

(4) A discussion of the identification of the victim as the individual *named* in the information is found in 86 *A.L.R.2d* 722 (by way of buttons, belts, bowleggedness, clothing, coins, glasses, feet, ferry tickets, fingerprints, hair, hairpins, height, keys, union card, laundry marks, letters, moles, knives, rings, scars, tattoos, teeth, a truss, a wallet, a watch and last, but certainly not least, a complete and full discussion of the old familiar doctrine of *idem sonans*).

(5) It is not error to deny a defense request for the production of photographs used in a pretrial identification.—*Simmons v. United States,* 390 U.S. 377, 19 L.Ed.2d 1247, 88 S.Ct. 967.

(6) A person may be identified by his size, height, movements, features, mannerisms and clothing.—*State v. Williamson,* 78 N.M. 751, 438 P.2d 161.

(7) To overcome the taint of a "bad" lineup, the state is required to show by "clear and convincing" proof that the in-court identifications are based upon observations other than at the lineup. "Clear and convincing" proof means clear, sufficient and unequivocal evidence or evidence which is so clear that it leaves no substantial doubt.—*People v. Caruso,* 65 Cal.Rptr. 336, 436 P.2d 336.

(8) *Wade* and *Gilbert* are to be applied prospectively only.—*People v. Caruso,* 65 Cal.Rptr. 336, 436 P.2d 336.

(9) The rights of an accused who was identified by an eyewitness while the accused was being unlawfully detained following his lawful arrest are adequately protected when the eyewitness takes the stand in open court for examination and cross-examination.—*People v. Stoner,* 55 Cal.Rptr. 897, 422 P.2d 585.

(10) Identification of a voice on the telephone may be proved circumstantially.—*Grogan v. United States,* 386 F.2d 300.

(11) The testimony of a third person who heard or observed an extrajudicial identification is admissible as an exception to the hearsay rule.—*People v. Pedercine,* 255 Cal.App.2d 363, 63 Cal.-Rptr. 873; *Gallegos v. People,* 157 Colo. 484, 403 P.2d 864.

(12) Permitting witnesses to point to a defendant in open court is not error.—*State v. Dunn,* 91 Idaho 870, 434 P.2d 88.

(13) A witness' identification of the defendant from the public portion of the courtroom on the day the case was set for trial did not preclude the same witness' later in-court identification.—*State v. Hunsucker,* 3 N.C.App. 281, 164 S.E.2d 507.

(14) There is no requirement that an accused be placed in a lineup to test the ability of the witnesses to identify him. In other words, he cannot demand that this be done.—*People v. Stewart,* 97 Ill.App.2d 378, 240 N.E.2d 146.

(15) Conducting a lineup without informing the defendant of his right to counsel does not throw out his conviction where none of the evidence produced at the trial resulted from the lineup.—*Caples v. United States*, 391 F.2d 1018.

(16) Where the victim of a crime is working with the police in an effort to identify the culprit from pictures it is not required that defense counsel for all those suspected or identified be present with the police and the victim.—*State v. Stamey*, 3 N.C.App. 200, 164 S.E.2d 547.

(17) The fact that the only reason the defendant was at the police station when he was identified by the victim was that he was unlawfully arrested did not preclude admissibility of the victim's station house identification.—*Parks v. State*, 4 Md.App. 432, 243 A.2d 645.

(18) Showing a photograph of the defendant to a witness before his in-court identification is not in violation of the constitution where there is no evidence that the picture was used to prime the witness or to bolster an otherwise shaky identification.—*People v. Smith*, 259 Cal.App.2d 814, 66 Cal.Rptr. 551.

IMPEACHMENT

(1) Evidence of prior inconsistent statements to impeach the defendant may be considered not only for the purpose of testing the defendant's credibility but with all other evidence in determining his guilt.—*People v. Underwood*, 37 Cal.Rptr. 313, 389 P.2d 937.

(2) The impeachment of a witness by medical testimony that the witness is a liar is discussed in 15 *A.L.R.* 932.

(3) Even though the defendant is permitted to testify at his trial on the limited issue of the voluntariness of his confession, he may be impeached by prior felony convictions.—*Boone v. State*, 2 Md.App. 80, 233 A.2d 476.

(4) Where the defendant was given probation on condition that he spend the first ten months in the county jail, the condition did not render the crime a misdemeanor.—*People v. Esparza,* 253 Cal.App.2d 362, 61 Cal.Rptr. 167.

(5) The fact that the witness is a convicted perjurer concerns only the credibility, not the competency, of his testimony.—*State v. Barick,* 143 Mont. 273, 389 P.2d 170.

(6) It is prejudicial to require the defense to request, receive and read *Jencks*-type "statements" in front of the jury.—*Gregory v. United States,* 369 F.2d 185.

(7) The mere fact that during his testimony a police officer tells the jury that he knew the defendant before he apprehended him does not indicate to the jury that the defendant has had prior trouble with the police.—*State v. Knicker,* 424 S.W.2d 605.

(8) Allowing witnesses to be impeached by their prior inconsistent statements does not deprive the defendant of any constitutional rights.—*Gaitan v. People,* 447 P.2d 1001.

(9) Homosexuality or an "unnatural relationship" is admissible if and when it shows the bias, interest or motive of a witness.—*People v. Rowland,* 69 Cal.Rptr. 269.

(10) Excluded evidence under the Fourth Amendment may be introduced for impeachment purposes.—*State v. Cannito,* 183 Neb. 575, 162 N.W.2d 260.

INDICTMENTS

(1) An indictment cannot be challenged on the ground of the inadequacy or incompetency of evidence before the grand jury.—*United States ex rel Almeida v. Rundle,* 383 F.2d 421.

(2) A "secret indictment" does not violate a defendant's constitutional rights.—*Haynes v. Gladden,* 422 P.2d 679.

(3) After an indictment is dismissed, the state may proceed on the same matter by complaint and information.—*Stabile v. Justice's Court of Las Vegas Township,* 83 Nev. 393, 432 P.2d 670.

(4) You may have separate counts of perjury committed at the same hearing.—*Seymour v. United States,* 77 F.2d 577.

(5) The short indictment form for murder (A murdered B) permitted the state to prove a felony-murder, a premeditated murder, or both.—*State v. Mayberry,* 52 N.J. 413, 245 A.2d 481.

INFORMATIONS

(1) A defendant who stands mute at his arraignment does not preserve any right to thereafter challenge the sufficiency of the information or the jurisdiction of the court.—*In re Pendygraft,* 438 P.2d 290.

(2) An information may be amended to add an offense shown to have been committed by the testimony at the preliminary examination; but the defense is entitled to a continuance to prepare its case.—*People v. Sipult,* 44 Cal.Rptr. 846, 243 Cal.App.2d 862.

(3) "(A)n information that charges in a single count that the defendant did all of the forbidden things, by employing the conjunction 'and' where the statute uses 'or,' is good, and is supported by proof that the defendant committed the offense in any of the ways specified."—*Rowe v. People,* 26 Colo. 542, 59 Pac. 57.

(4) Even though the state's witnesses testified at the preliminary examination that the burglary occurred on August 8, a court need not grant the defendant another preliminary examination

when it is shown that the burglary really took place on September 8 and the defendant does not show he was prejudiced in any way.—*State v. Robertson*, 190 Kan. 720, 378 P.2d 66.

(5) An information charging murder also charges all lesser offenses necessarily included in the crime of murder, and this includes voluntary and involuntary manslaughter.—*In re McCartney*, 51 Cal.Rptr. 894, 415 P.2d 782.

(6) A complaining witness has no control over the prosecution of a case and can neither require a prosecution nor a dismissal.—*People v. Dennis*, 433 P.2d 339.

(7) The right to be furnished a copy of the information 24 hours prior to pleading is a statutory right which may be waived. —*State v. Bargas*, 77 N.M. 764, 427 P.2d 273.

(8) The endorsement of the names of additional witnesses on an information after a mistrial had been granted does not constitute an amendment to the information or entitle the defendant to a rearraignment.—*State v. Mader*, 196 Kan. 469, 412 P.2d 1001.

(9) Where it is shown to a trial court that the defendant has been denied a constitutional right at his preliminary examination, the trial court must abate the information until there has been a proper preliminary examination. The proper course is to remand the accused to the magistrate for such an examination. The trial court does not lose jurisdiction of the information and the filing of a new information (after the defendant is once again held for trial) is not required.—*State v. Vaughn*, 74 N.M. 365, 393 P.2d 711.

(10) Where several acts can constitute a single crime, an information may charge the crime in one count and the commission of the crime by alternative acts in the same count.—*State v. Scott*, 64 Wash.2d 992, 395 P.2d 377.

(11) If the amended information materially changes the information, the defendant must be rearraigned.—*Hanley v. Zenoff*, 81 Nev. 7, 398 P.2d 241.

(12) One count of an information may, by reference, incorporate allegations in another count if the reference is clear and specific.—*Martinez v. People,* 431 P.2d 765.

(13) "Possession of narcotics" is not necessarily included in the charge of "offering to sell narcotics" because it is possible to offer narcotics for sale without having actual or constructive possession of the narcotic.—*People v. Blunt,* 50 Cal.Rptr. 440, 241 Cal.-App.2d 200.

(14) A charge of assault with intent to commit rape includes the crime of attempt to rape.—*State v. Hall,* 88 Idaho 117, 397 P.2d 261.

(15) You may have separate counts of perjury committed at the same hearing.—*Seymour v. United States,* 77 F.2d 577.

(16) Where a "prior" is an essential element of the crime presently charged, it is referred to in the pleading, is read to the jury, must be proved and may be mentioned in argument.—*People v. Shaw,* 46 Cal.Rptr. 217.

(17) After an indictment is dismissed, the state may proceed on the same matter by complaint and information.—*Stabile v. Justice's Court of Las Vegas Township,* 83 Nev. 393, 432 P.2d 670.

(18) A charge of receiving need not allege the name of the person from whom the defendant received the property.—*Wertheimer v. State,* 201 Ind. 572, 169 N.E. 40, 68 *A.L.R.* 178.

(19) Although the defendant entered a plea of not guilty, a dismissal thereafter did not constitute an acquittal and further prosecution was not prohibited on the theory of double jeopardy. —*State v. Rhodes,* 76 N.M. 177, 413 P.2d 214.

(20) The defendant waives any irregularities in his preliminary examination when he pleads guilty in district court or not guilty and goes to trial on the information.—*Cleveland v. State,* 195 Kan. 544, 407 P.2d 488.

(21) When a hit-and-run statute is silent as to where the offense must occur, it is not necessary to allege or prove that the offense occurred on a public highway.—*People v. Stansberry,* 51 Cal.-Rptr. 403, 242 Cal.App.2d 199.

(22) The short indictment form for murder (A murdered B) permitted the state to prove a felony-murder, a premeditated murder, or both.—*State v. Mayberry,* 52 N.J. 413, 245 A.2d 481.

INJURIES

(1) The admissibility, in a prosecution for an assault or a similar offense involving physical violence, of the extent or effect of the victim's injuries is discussed in 87 *A.L.R.2d* 926 (display of the bare back of the victim in a shotgun case, the length of time the victim was in the hospital, that the victim had to have x-rays taken, that now when the victim stooped over he got dizzy, that trouble with the victim's sight developed the day after the assault, and that the lacerations would cause permanent scars).

(2) Allowing the pathologist who performed the autopsy on the victim of a vehicular manslaughter to answer a hypothetical question on the cause of the injuries was not error.—*State v. Wade,* 159 N.W.2d 396.

INSANITY

(1) The chronic addiction to alcohol is not legal insanity. An alcoholic is held to the same standards of responsibility as any-one else.—*City of Seattle v. Hill,* 435 P.2d 692.

(2) An insanity expert may not give an opinion which is based in part on information coming to him from others.—175 *A.L.R.* 274.

(3) An instruction that "irresistible impulse" is not a test for sanity is proper where there is testimony indicating that the defendant responded to such an impulse.—*State v. Coltharp,* 199 Kan. 598, 433 P.2d 418.

(4) A doctor, in arriving at his opinion on insanity, may use materials gathered from psychological tests given by psychologists under his direction.—*State v. Coltharp,* 199 Kan. 598, 433 P.2d 418.

(5) In a sex case it may be permissible to introduce psychiatric testimony concerning the mental and emotional condition of the "victim."—*Ballard v. Superior Court of San Diego County,* 49 Cal.Rptr. 302, 410 P.2d 838.

(6) A prejudice against the defense of insanity will not disqualify one from sitting as a juror where the nature of the prejudice is such that the court is satisfied that it will not influence the juror's verdict.—*State v. Baker,* 74 Mo. 292, 41 Am.Rep. 314, 112 *A.L.R.* 532.

(7) The M'Naughton test ("right" from "wrong") means "morally wrong."—*People v. Schmidt,* 216 N.Y. 324, 110 N.E. 945.

(8) Where the defendant's psychiatric testimony indicates insanity, but the state's lay witness testimony supports a verdict of sanity, the defendant is not entitled to a directed verdict of not guilty by reason of insanity if the lay evidence has an adequate foundation.—*People v. Wax,* 75 Ill.App.2d 163, 220 N.E.2d 600.

(9) The examination of a defendant by psychiatrists for the prosecuting attorney without the defendant's counsel being present (or any notice being given to him) does not violate the constitutional rights of the defendant.—*Blocker v. State,* 92 Fla. 878, 110 So. 547. Also *Walters v. State,* 22 Ala.App. 644, 119 So. 248 (where court ordered it done); *State v. Myers,* 220 S.C. 309, 67 S.E.2d 506.

(10) A court ordered the defendant to be examined as to his sanity. The defendant answered the doctor's questions voluntarily. The court held that the testimony of the doctor was not violative of the defendant's right against self-incrimination or of the due process clause of the Fourteenth Amendment. The court further held that the trial court could order such an examination but it could not force the defendant to engage in the examination against his will. If the defendant was forced to engage in the examination or forced to consent to it through trickery, the doctor's evidence could not be used against the defendant. The court also said that it was proper for the state to ask the doctor if he was appointed by the court to examine the defendant.—*Hunt v. State,* 248 Ala. 217, 27 So.2d 180. Also *Comm'th v. Musto,* 348 Pa. 300, 35 A.2d 307 (not really court order here, just consent by court to state's attorney to have it done before trial).

(11) A defendant's constitutional rights are not violated by refusing to let his counsel be with him during a mental examination.—*United States v. Albright,* 388 F.2d 719.

(12) A delay to determine the defendant's mental capacity to stand trial is "good cause" for continuing the trial past the 60-day limit.—*People v. McGill,* 65 Cal.Rptr. 482, 257 A.C.A. 859.

(13) A sanity hearing does not have to be held before the same judge who ordered the hearing.—*People v. Hill,* 60 Cal.Rptr. 234, 429 P.2d 586.

(14) Where a defendant is charged with murder and is committed to the state asylum before trial, it is not violative of the defendant's right against self-incrimination to have a doctor from the state asylum testify as to the defendant's sanity.—*Hunt v. State,* 248 Ala. 217, 27 S.2d 186.

(15) Where a court orders the defendant to be examined at the state's request, the defendant does not become a witness against himself when the doctor testifies.—*State v. Petty,* 32 Nev. 384, 108 Pac. 934. Also *People v. Bundy,* 168 Cal. 777, 145 Pac. 537.

(16) Where the mental competency of the defendant is before a magistrate at or prior to the preliminary examination, the magistrate should bind the defendant over and the competency issue should be determined by the trial court after a determination by the court that there was probable cause.—*State v. McCredden*, 33 Wis.2d 661, 148 N.W.2d 33.

(17) Where a psychiatrist interviewed the defendant at the request of the state, the psychiatrist was an agent of the state with no more right than any such agent to elicit admissions from the defendant without his being informed of his rights, and his admissions of guilt to the psychiatrist should have been excluded.—*People v. Polk*, 44 Cal.Rptr. 773, 402 P.2d 845.

(18) A case history related by the defendant to a doctor called only for diagnosis and not treatment, is not admissible.—65 *A.L.R.* 1217; 175 *A.L.R.* 274.

(19) Evidence tending to establish sanity may be introduced by the state in its case in chief; but it does not have to.—*Henderson v. People*, 156 Colo. 229, 397 P.2d 872.

(20) Where a doctor was sent by the state solely for the purpose of examining the accused in order to report upon his sanity, the relation of physician and patient did not exist between the doctor and the accused.—*State v. Fouquette*, 67 Nev. 505, 221 P.2d 404.

(21) Where the defendant's expert insanity witness testified that the defendant was "characteristically a passive man," the state was allowed to show the defendant's reputation in the community for being quarrelsome.—*State v. Johnson*, 69 Wash.2d 264, 418 P.2d 238.

(22) The validity and construction of statutes providing for a psychiatric examination of an accused to determine his mental condition are discussed in 32 *A.L.R.2d* 439.

(23) The testimony of a coroner, physician or layman who visited and observed the defendant in jail is not privileged and those observations are admissible. The court noted that the manner in which the defendant occupied himself while in jail is relevant on an insanity issue.—*State v. Genna,* 163 La. 701, 112 So. 655.

(24) The physician-patient privilege does not apply to the testimony of a physician who examined the defendant for the purpose of commitment.—*People v. Lipscomb,* 69 Cal.Rptr. 127, 263 A.C.A. 61.

(25) Permitting a prosecution psychiatrist to sit in the courtroom and listen to a defense psychiatrist and then testify on rebuttal even though the "witness rule" (exclusion) had been invoked was not error.—*Wallace v. State,* 447 P.2d 30.

(26) The jury may disbelieve the testimony of a psychiatrist.—*People v. Scott,* 11 Mich.App. 576, 161 N.W.2d 753.

INSTRUCTIONS

(1) An instruction stating that a presumption of law is raised that every man intends the natural and probable consequences of his voluntary acts does no harm to the traditional presumption of innocence.—*State v. Alvis,* 70 Wash.2d 969, 425 P.2d 924.

(2) Once there is proof of the defendant's use of fictitious names, the state is entitled to an instruction that the use of fictitious names may be considered as bearing on guilt.—*State v. Inzerillo,* 191 Kan. 586, 383 P.2d 546.

(3) A jury need not be instructed that the uncorroborated testimony of a police narcotics officer must be viewed with suspicion and acted upon with caution, or that such a rule is applicable to new recruits or novice officers.—*Bush v. United States,* 375 F.2d 602.

(4) It is proper to refuse to instruct that police officers are not as likely to tell the truth as other witnesses.—*Battese v. State,* 425 P.2d 606.

(5) Erroneous instructions may be withdrawn even after the jury has retired to deliberate.—*State v. O'Keefe,* 45 Hawaii 368, 367 P.2d 91.

(6) A court may recall jurors for further instructions even after they have begun deliberations.—*People v. Wester,* 45 Cal.Rptr. 114.

(7) An instruction that self-defense is not available to a defendant who was the aggressor or the one who provoked the affray is not a comment on the evidence.—*State v. Goldstein,* 65 Wash.2d 901, 400 P.2d 368.

(8) The necessity of a court charging upon motive in a homicide case is discussed in 71 *A.L.R.2d* 1025.

(9) The giving of an instruction in a sodomy prosecution in the language of the statute is not prejudicial, even though the statute includes the language "detestable and abominable crime against nature."—*Johnson v. State,* 380 P.2d 284.

(10) An instruction that it is not necessary to prove that the assault charged was committed on the exact date alleged in the indictment and that it is sufficient if the prosecutor establishes that it occurred within the statutory period of limitations is not erroneous.—*State v. Gibbons,* 228 Ore. 238, 364 P.2d 611.

(11) An instruction telling the jury that they may consider the defendant's refusal to take a breathalyzer test is proper.—*People v. Sudduth,* 55 Cal.Rptr. 393, 421 P.2d 401.

(12) An instruction cautioning the jury to disregard statements, objections and comments of the court and counsel and evidentiary rulings of the court and admonishing the jury that instructions must be read as a whole is not error.—*Jordan v. People,* 161 Colo. 54, 419 P.2d 656.

(13) An instruction that if the jury finds exculpatory statements of the defendant untrue, they may be considered as evidence of his consciousness of guilt does not violate the Fifth or Sixth Amendments.—*United States v. Smith,* 379 F.2d 628.

(14) An instruction telling the jury their function in regard to the "habitual criminal statute" and the posture of the case when that point has been reached is not a comment on the evidence.—*State v. Bryant,* 437 P.2d 398.

(15) A court has the duty to declare facts judicially noticed to a jury before the jury may base its verdict upon such facts.—*State v. Jones,* 240 Ore. 129, 400 P.2d 524.

(16) The mere fact that a defendant may have been drinking prior to the commission of a crime does not establish intoxication or require the giving of such an instruction.—*People v. Miller,* 22 Cal.Rptr. 465, 372 P.2d 297.

(17) Even though not requested, the trial court must instruct the jury that one of the essential elements of robbery is an intent to steal.—*People v. Ford,* 36 Cal.Rptr. 620, 388 P.2d 892.

(18) An instruction on flight was proper even though the defendant did not flee until a week after the crime.—*State v. Bryant,* 437 P.2d 398.

(19) It is error for a trial court to give an instruction attempting to define reasonable doubt.—*Wilson v. State,* 403 P.2d 262.

(20) "The doctrine of reasonable doubt applies to proof of guilt and not to the establishment of each incident or event inculpating the defendant."—*People v. Klinkenberg,* 90 Cal.App.2d 608, 204 P.2d 47; *People v. Kross,* 112 Cal.App.2d 602, 247 P.2d 44.

(21) An instruction on the defendant's failure to explain his possession of recently stolen property is not improper.—*People v. DeLeon,* 46 Cal.Rptr. 241, 236 Cal.App.2d 530; but see *Payne v. State,* 435 P.2d 424.

INTOXICATION

(1) An officer's observations of symptoms of the defendant's drunkenness observed by the officer when he came upon the defendant slumped over the steering wheel of his car in a ditch off the highway were admissible though the officer had no authority to arrest the defendant for drunk driving without a warrant.—*Puckett v. State,* 363 P.2d 953.

(2) The mere fact that a defendant may have been drinking prior to the commission of a crime does not establish that he was intoxicated or require the giving of such an instruction.—*People v. Miller,* 22 Cal.Rptr. 465, 372 P.2d 297.

(3) One who voluntarily drinks himself into unconsciousness intends whatever the foreseeable consequences or inevitable results of such intoxication are, and that intent may be sufficient for second-degree murder.—*Watkins v. People,* 158 Colo. 485, 408 P.2d 425.

(4) Chronic addiction to alcohol is not legal insanity. An alcoholic is held to the same standards of responsibility as anyone else.—*City of Seattle v. Hill,* 435 P.2d 692.

(5) "Unless a defendant's intoxication amounts to a mania—that is, unless he is so drunk as to be unconscious of the meaning of his words—his intoxication does not render inadmissible his confession of facts tending to incriminate him. The extent of his intoxication when the confession was made, however, is a relevant circumstance bearing upon its credibility, a question exclusively for the jury's determination."—*State v. Logner,* 266 N.C. 238, 145 S.E.2d 867.

(6) An instruction telling the jury that they may consider the defendant's refusal to take a breathalyzer test is proper.—*People v. Sudduth,* 55 Cal.Rptr. 393, 421 P.2d 401.

JEOPARDY

(1) An increased sentence on retrial or a denial of credit for that part of the invalid sentence already served is a violation of the double jeopardy clause of the United States Constitution.—*Patton v. State of N.C.*, 381 F.2d 636.

(2) In determining whether the defendant can successfully plead double jeopardy, the trial court may look to the entire record of the former trial and is not restricted to the indictment or information alone.—*Price v. State,* 437 P.2d 330.

(3) A defendant may be prosecuted for driving while intoxicated in a district court after the state has entered a nolle prosequi in justice court because a jury trial was demanded on the same charge.—*State v. Sweat,* 78 N.M. 512, 433 P.2d 229.

(4) Although a defendant entered a plea of not guilty, a dismissal on motion of the state thereafter did not constitute an acquittal and further prosecution was not prohibited on the theory of double jeopardy.—*State v. Rhodes,* 76 N.M. 177, 413 P.2d 214.

(5) The defendant who was convicted of violating a city ordinance prohibiting the carrying of a concealed weapon was not placed in double jeopardy when he was subsequently convicted in a county court under a statute prohibiting certain convicted felons from carrying pistols as a result of the same incident.—*Earwood v. State,* 198 Kan. 659, 426 P.2d 151.

(6) The plea of double jeopardy is not available after a mistrial where the defendant has moved for the mistrial.—*State v. Wolak,* 33 N.J. 419, 165 A.2d 177.

(7) A defendant who pleaded guilty to a charge of driving an automobile without having his operator's license in his immediate possession when he knew he was not guilty, for the express purpose of immunizing himself against further prosecution for the more serious offense of driving at a time when his operator's license had been revoked procured his "conviction" and foreclosed himself from urging double jeopardy.—*Hampton v. Municipal Court of Pasadena Judicial Dist., Los Angeles County,* 51 Cal.Rptr. 760, 242 Cal.App.2d 689.

(8) An acquittal on a charge of transporting narcotics does not prohibit a prosecution for the possession of the narcotics allegedly transported.—*People v. Webb,* 52 Cal.Rptr. 495.

(9) The dismissal of a charge by a magistrate at a preliminary examination is not res judicata and a second charge may be filed. —*People v. Joseph,* 153 Cal.App.2d 548, 314 P.2d 1004. Also *People v. Prewitt,* 52 Cal.2d 330, 341 P.2d 1 (where the magistrate threw it out because he concluded the evidence was illegally seized).

(10) The defendant was not put in jeopardy when he was tried for escape after he was punished for the escape by jail authorities by being put in isolation.—*State v. Vinson,* 8 Ariz.App. 93, 443 P.2d 700.

(11) A reversal on appeal is not a bar to a retrial of the reversed case.—*State v. Bloomer,* 197 Kan. 668, 421 P.2d 58.

(12) Jeopardy attaches in a criminal prosecution tried to the court at that point when the presentation of proof begins.—*McCoy v. District Court In and For City and County of Denver,* 156 Colo. 115, 397 P.2d 733.

(13) A mistrial following a hung jury is not a bar to further prosecution even though the jury hung 10 for acquittal, 2 for guilt on a lesser charge.—*People v. Griffin,* 58 Cal.Rptr. 107, 426 P.2d 507.

(14) The dismissal of a felony prosecution by the state (before jeopardy had attached) is not a bar to filing a new action on the same charge.—*People v. Hernandez,* 58 Cal.Rptr. 835, 250 Cal.-App.2d 842.

(15) Possession of narcotics is not necessarily included in the charge of offering to sell narcotics because it is possible to offer narcotics for sale without having actual or constructive possession of the narcotic.—*People v. Blunt,* 50 Cal.Rptr. 440, 241 Cal.-App.2d 200.

(16) Defendant was not put twice in jeopardy when the prosecution used his 1960 conviction to increase the penalty on his current conviction.—*Anderson v. Wilson,* 397 F.2d 255.

JUDGMENTS

(1) The judgment in a criminal case is complete and valid when it is orally pronounced and entered in the minutes. There is no requirement that it be written.—*Application of Anderson,* 6 Ariz.-App. 563, 435 P.2d 70.

JUDICIAL NOTICE

(1) An appeals court may take judicial notice of boundaries of counties of the state and of the geographical locations of cities and towns within the state.—*Morris v. State,* 363 P.2d 377.

(2) A court may judicially notice that the business of a bank was at its heaviest from 5:00 to 6:00 P.M.—*People v. Green,* 44 Cal.Rptr. 438, 234 Cal.App.2d 871.

(3) Judicial notice may be taken of fact that today's automobiles are capable of high speeds and that reckless individuals often press their vehicles to the maximum. (That seems like quite a milestone!)—*People v. Heckard,* 431 P.2d 1014.

(4) State courts may take judicial notice of the regulations of the departments of state governments and regulations established by "important" state boards and commissions. (I have no cases defining "important," however.)—*Drillon v. Ind. Accident Commn.,* 110 P.2d 64; *Ariz. Climate Control, Inc., v. Hill,* 86 Ariz. 180, 342 P.2d 854.

(5) A reviewing court may take judicial notice of anything the court of original jurisdiction may properly notice.—*People v. Melchor,* 47 Cal.Rptr. 235, 237 Cal.App.2d 685.

(6) A court has the duty to declare facts judicially noticed to a jury before the jury may base its verdict upon such facts.—*State v. Jones,* 240 Ore. 129, 400 P.2d 524.

(7) Judicial notice may be taken of the fact that property has "some" value.—*People v. Tassone,* 41 Ill. 227, 241 N.E.2d 419.

JURISDICTION

(1) A court has jurisdiction to try a defendant even though he was forcibly brought to the jurisdiction after an abortive extradition proceeding.—*Call v. State,* 195 Kan. 668, 408 P.2d 668.

(2) "The power of a court to try a person for crime is not impaired by the fact that he had been brought within the court's jurisdiction by reason of a 'forcible abduction.'"—*Frisbie v. Collins,* 284 F.2d 135, 342 U.S. 519, 522, 72 S.Ct. 509, 511, 96 L.Ed 541.

(3) Where a prior conviction (charged) makes the offense a felony, the offense charged does not become a misdemeanor when the prior conviction is admitted and the defendant is still subject

to imprisonment as a felon and the offense is cognizable in superior court.—*People v. Shaw,* 46 Cal.Rptr. 217.

(4) The suspension of an operator's license upon a conviction for reckless driving is not a "penalty" in the sense that it puts cognizance of such an offense out of the hands of a justice court and into a superior court.—*State v. Pruett,* 91 Idaho 537, 428 P.2d 43.

(5) A citizen of the United States may be punished in the United States for conspiring to smuggle amphetamine tablets into the United States even though the acts leading to the crime were committed in Mexico.—*Brulay v. United States,* 383 F.2d 345.

(6) In habeas corpus, prohibition or certiorari proceedings, "jurisdiction" is not limited to its fundamental meaning, and judicial acts may be restrained or annulled if it is determined that they are in excess of a court's powers as defined by the constitution, a statute or court rules.—*In re Zerbe,* 36 Cal.Rptr. 286, 388 P.2d 182.

(7) The Fourth Amendment guarantees do not apply to things seized by Mexican officers in Mexico (not under the direction of U.S. police) and such evidence is admissible in a United States court (apparently even though seized by Mexican police under what the United States would call unlawful conditions).—*Brulay v. United States,* 383 F.2d 345.

(8) The violation of a statute making it a crime for any officer having custody of a defendant after arrest to deny that defendant's request to communicate with an attorney does not require the dismissal of the charge against the defendant.—*State v. Roderick,* 243 Ore. 105, 412 P.2d 17.

JURY & JURORS

(1) A jury view is not evidence, but it does assist the jury in comprehending the evidence.—*Spillers v. State,* 436 P.2d 18.

(2) Jurors may not be asked about their religious affiliations.—*State v. Huff,* 14 N.J. 240, 102 A.2d 8, 54 *A.L.R.2d* 1215.

(3) Although jurors may take notes, a lack of notes does not render the defendant's trial an unfair one.—*Skinner v. State,* 83 Nev. 380, 432 P.2d 675.

(4) The effect of the use of handbooks by the court to indoctrinate jurors is discussed in 89 *A.L.R.2d* 197.

(5) The state may exercise a peremptory challenge after it stated it was satisfied with the jury as long as there is no showing of prejudice.—*People v. Mitchell,* 38 Cal.Rptr. 726, 392 P.2d 526.

(6) A prejudice against the defense of insanity will not disqualify one from sitting as a juror where the nature of the prejudice is such that the court is satisfied that it will not influence the juror's verdict.—*State v. Baker,* 74 Mo. 292, 41 Am.Rep. 314, 112 *A.L.R.* 532.

(7) There is no requirement that a jury deliberate for any particular period of time.—*Wall v. United States,* 384 F.2d 758.

(8) The effect a hasty or short verdict has on a conviction is discussed in 91 *A.L.R.2d* 1238.

(9) Whether to replay all or part of the testimony for the jury is within the discretion of the trial court.—*Price v. State,* 437 P.2d 330.

(10) The jury may be told that a codefendant has pleaded guilty.—*United States v. Restaino,* 369 F.2d 544.

(11) A court has the duty to declare facts judicially noticed to a jury before the jury may base its verdict upon such facts.—*State v. Jones,* 240 Ore. 129, 400 P.2d 524.

(12) Erroneous instructions may be withdrawn even if jury has retired to deliberate.—*State v. O'Keefe,* 45 Hawaii 368, 367 P.2d 91.

(13) A court may recall jurors for further instructions.—*People v. Wester,* 45 Cal.Rptr. 114.

(14) Where exemplars and the questioned writing are in evidence a comparison may be made by the jury with or without the aid of the handwriting expert's testimony and the results of the comparisons are a matter for the jury.—*Kidd v. Hillman,* 14 Cal.App.2d 507, 58 P.2d 662; *People v. Weiskopf,* 60 Cal.App.2d 214, 140 P.2d 201; *People v. Horowitz,* 70 Cal.App.2d 675, 161 P.2d 833, 80 *A.L.R.2d* 272, 275, 276, 277.

(15) Where a "prior" is an essential element of the crime presently charged, it is referred to in the pleading, is read to the jury, must be proved and may be mentioned in argument.—*People v. Shaw,* 46 Cal.Rptr. 217.

(16) The defendant was not denied a fair trial where the judge talked to a juror in chambers about her request to be excused because of emotional distress and then excused the juror in open court in front of the defendant.—*In re Lessard,* 62 C.2d 497, 42 Cal.Rptr. 583, 399 P.2d 39.

(17) The inattention of jurors is discussed in 88 *A.L.R.2d* 1275 (where jurors who sleep, doze, drowse, have chills, hang their heads and perform other rude acts are discussed).

(18) Misconduct of a juror which will authorize or require the withdrawal of the juror is discussed in 86 *A.L.R.* 928 (where a juror was found wandering the streets in a drunken condition, where a foreman pointed to another juror and said "this man here would like to have further instructions," and where one juror applauded when the court made a misstatement of the law).

(19) The prosecution's use of a "jury list" does not deprive the accused of a fair trial.—*People v. Airheart,* 68 Cal.Rptr. 857, 262 A.C.A. 728.

(20) A prosecutor's question of the jurors if any of them had beliefs against capital punishment does not violate any of the defendant's constitutional rights.—*Curtis v. State,* 4 Md.App. 499, 243 A.2d 656.

(21) There is no right on the part of the defendant to have minor witnesses questioned as to their competency outside the presence of the jury.—*Ramer v. State,* 40 Wis.2d 79, 161 N.W.2d 209.

(22) The jury may disbelieve the testimony of a pychiatrist.—*People v. Scott,* 11 Mich.App. 576, 161 N.W. 2d 753.

KIDNAPPING

(1) When a robbery occurs during a kidnapping, the crime becomes "kidnapping for robbery" from the beginning whether or not the kidnapper originally intended to rob the victim.—*In re Ward,* 51 Cal.Rptr. 272, 414 P.2d 400.

(2) Where the kidnapping occurs after the robbery it is still "kidnapping for robbery" if there is a reasonable inference that the victim was transported to effect the escape of the robber or to take the victim to some place where he could not easily sound an alarm.—*People v. Martin,* 58 Cal.Rptr. 481, 250 Cal.App.2d 263.

(3) Injuries sustained by a kidnapping victim when he escaped from the kidnapper by jumping from a truck were not the type of "bodily harms" contemplated by the statute increasing the penalty for kidnapping if the victim suffered "bodily harm."—*People v. Baker,* 41 Cal.Rptr. 696, 231 Cal.App.2d 301.

(4) The defendant's offering a 14-year-old child a job and requesting that she come with him to his office when he had no office and was unemployed, constituted "enticing away," within a statute defining second-degree kidnapping as "leading, taking, enticing away or detaining a child under age 16 with intent to conceal him from his parents." There is no requirement of an actual concealment.—*State v. Missmer,* 435 P.2d 683.

(5) Removal for 100 to 150 feet and detention for 5 minutes during an indecent assault was "kidnapping."—*State v. Morris,* 160 N.W.2d 715.

LETTERS

(1) The admission into evidence of a letter written by the defendant while in prison and handled as a piece of mail by the prison authorities was not an invasion of the defendant's privacy and not error.—*Hayes v. United States,* 367 F.2d 216.

LIE DETECTOR

(1) The state is bound by its promise to dismiss a prosecution if the defendant passes a lie-detector test.—*Florida v. Davis,* 188 So.2d 24.

(2) The fact that before confessing the defendant took a polygraph and that the operator told the defendant he thought he was not telling the truth does not show any inherent coercion requiring the exclusion of the confession.—*People v. Barreto,* 64 Cal.Rptr. 211, 256 Cal.App.2d 392.

LIMINE

(1) Motions in limine (which are really pretrial motions to suppress) are discussed in 94 *A.L.R.2d* 1082 (covering those areas where a ruling is sought to exclude certain evidence which one side believes prejudicial and about to be introduced).

(2) The granting of a motion to suppress is not appealable.—*Ballard v. Superior Court, San Diego County,* 44 Cal.Rptr. 291.

(3) A trial judge is not bound by a pretrial denial of a motion to suppress.—*Washington v. United States,* 401 F.2d 915.

(4) A defendant is not entitled to a separate trial on each issue. —*State v. Forcella,* 52 N.J. 263, 245 A.2d 181. (Phew! That's good to know.)

LIMITATIONS

(1) The defendant who had originally been charged with murder, then convicted of manslaughter, got this conviction reversed, could be retried for manslaughter on the original information, even though the period of limitations for manslaughter had run out where the information had originally been filed in time.—*In re McCartney,* 51 Cal.Rptr. 894, 415 P.2d 782.

(2) A defendant may be convicted of a felony-murder even though, at the time of the trial, the felony has been barred by the statute of limitations.—*People v. Lilliock,* 71 Cal.Rptr. 434, 265 A.C.A. 465.

MALICE

(1) First-degree murder requires express malice; murder second consists of implied malice.—*Ingles v. People,* 92 Colo. 518, 22 P.2d 1109.

(2) Although one who commits euthanasia bears no ill will toward his victim and believes that his act is morally justified, he nevertheless acts with malice if he is able to comprehend that society prohibits his act regardless of his belief.—*People v. Conley,* 49 Cal.Rptr. 815, 411 P.2d 911.

(3) An actual intent to kill is not necessary for second-degree murder.—*Jackson v. Superior Court,* 42 Cal.Rptr. 838, 399 P.2d 374.

MANSLAUGHTER

(1) A drag racer can be charged as a principal in a mortor-vehicle manslaughter case although his car was not involved in the collision.—*Jacobs v. State,* 184 So.2d 711.

(2) When a hit-and-run statute is silent as to where the offense must have occurred, it is not necessary to allege or prove that the offense occurred on a public highway.—*People v. Stansberry,* 51 Cal.Rptr. 403, 242 Cal.App.2d 199.

(3) Allowing the pathologist who performed the autopsy on the victim of a vehicular manslaughter to answer a hypothetical question on the cause of the injuries was not error.—*State v. Wade,* 159 N.W.2d 396.

MOTION PICTURES

(1) Expert testimony that motion picture films showing the defendant beating a person were not retouched, showed no use of cosmetics and accurately represented the scene before the camera, sufficiently authenticated the films to render them admissible.—*People v. Samuels,* 58 Cal.Rptr. 439, 250 Cal.App.2d 501.

MURDER-FELONY

(1) The murder-felony doctrine applies to a case where the victim dies of fright during the course of a robbery (heart attack).—*State v. McKeiver,* 213 A.2d 320.

(2) The murder-felony doctrine applies even though the killing precedes the felony.—*State v. Hauptmann,* 115 N.J.L. 412, 180 Atl.809; *State v. Burzette,* 208 Iowa 818, 222 N.W. 394 (burglary), *Lemth v. Lawrence,* 282 Pa. 128, 127 Atl.465; *People v. Buss,* 210 Cal. 245, 290 Pac. 881; *People v. Dowell,* 204 Cal. 109, 266 Pac. 807; *People v. Kendrick,* 56 Cal.2d 71, 363 P.2d 13.

(3) "Obstructing" an officer is a felony that may be inherently dangerous to life calling for the application of the murder-felony rule.—*Brooks v. Superior Court of Los Angeles County,* 48 Cal.-Rptr. 762, 239 Cal.App.2d 538.

(4) The murder-felony rule does not extend to a nondangerous felony (like theft by false pretenses).—*People v. Phillips,* 42 Cal.Rptr. 868.

(5) Murder is of the first degree when committed during a robbery even if the killing is purely accidental.—*People v. Riser,* 47 C.2d 566, 305 P.2d 1.

(6) Where the defendant attempted a robbery inside the building and a fight started between him (and his companion) and the victim which carried out onto the sidewalk where the victim retrieved the money and the defendant stabbed and killed him, the murder-felony rule was applicable; this was all one continuous transaction.—*Payne v. State,* 81 Nev. 503, 406 P.2d 922.

(7) Under the murder-felony rule, it makes no difference if the felony intended is an integral ingredient of the murder—like an intent to assault the victim.—*People v. Talbot,* 51 Cal.Rptr. 417, 414 P.2d 633.

(8) Where two conspired to rob, a homicide by one while committing the robbery was within the common purpose and attributable to both.—*State v. Jensen,* 209 Ore. 239, 296 P.2d 618.

(9) If the murder takes place while the defendant is carrying a firearm in violation of a statute which prohibits convicted felons from carrying firearms, the murder-felony rule applies and it is murder in the second degree.—*People v. Schader,* 44 Cal.Rptr. 193, 401 P.2d 665.

(10) A homocide which is a direct and causal result of the commission of a felony inherently dangerous to human life, other than the felonies enumerated in the murder-felony statute, is second-degree murder.—*People v. Ford,* 36 Cal.Rptr. 620, 388 P.2d 892.

(11) A defendant may be convicted of a felony-murder even though, at the time of the trial, the felony has been barred by the statute of limitations.—*People v. Lilliock,* 71 Cal.Rptr. 434, 265 A.C.A. 465.

(12) The short indictment form for murder (A murdered B) permitted the state to prove a felony-murder, a premeditated murder, or both.—*State v. Mayberry,* 52 N.J. 413, 245 A.2d 481.

MUTUAL COMBAT

(1) "Mere fist fight or scuffle is not mutual combat. It usually means an encounter with deadly weapons in which the death of either or both of the parties is imminent. Such a combat must be mutual; both parties must be armed with deadly or dangerous weapons and have a mutual intention to use them. In this case the undisputed evidence shows that the accused had a deadly weapon, a loaded pistol, concealed on his person and that the person shot and seriously wounded had no weapon of any kind in his hands or on his person. The two men had a sudden quarrel and a scuffle, the defendant was pulled down on the floor by the other man, the defendant falling underneath the other man, and immediately the defendant drew his pistol and shot the man in his face. Under these facts we are of the opinion that the law of mutual combat was not involved."—*Watson v. State,* 66 Ga.App. 242, 17 S.E.2d 559.

NARCOTICS

(1) A police officer was permitted to testify that a one-inch "roach" found on the floorboard of an automobile was marijuana. —*People v. Perez,* 66 Cal.Rptr. 473, 259 Cal.App.2d 571.

(2) Paregoric is a narcotic drug.—*Browne v. State,* 24 Wis.2d 491, 131 N.W.2d 169.

(3) A police officer was allowed to testify as to whether the lack of visible scars on someone's arms would indicate whether he had been using heroin by way of an intravenous injection.—*People v. Cruz,* 66 Cal.Rptr. 772, 260 Cal.App.2d 55.

(4) A person may be convicted of being "under the influence" of a narcotic drug without offending the constitution. This is no different than being punished for "using" a narcotic. Discussed in *Robinson v. Cal.,* 370 U.S. 660, 8 L.Ed.2d 758, 82 S.Ct. 1417.

(5) The mature stalk of the cannabis plant without the presence of resin is *not* a *narcotic* drug.—*People v. Lott,* 241 Ill.2d 188, 181 N.E.2d 112.

(6) "Possession of narcotics" is not necessarily included in the charge of "offering to sell narcotics" because it is possible to offer narcotics for sale without having actual or constructive possession of the narcotic.—*People v. Blunt,* 50 Cal.Rptr. 440, 241 Cal.App.-2d 200.

(7) To sustain a conviction for possessing narcotics, it need not be shown that defendant had exclusive possession of the premises on which the narcotics were found or actual physical possession of the narcotic; possession may be established jointly or through an agent.—*People v. Solorio,* 42 Cal.Rptr. 914, 232 Cal.App.2d 527.

(8) A lay witness who is sufficiently trained and experienced can testify to the reaction of users of drugs. Here the lay witness who was permitted to testify was an officer with two years on the narcotic squad, who had played the role of an addict while associating with users, who had special training in the use and methods of administering narcotics, who had been taught to observe users and their reactions and who had observed twenty to thirty people under the influence of heroin and withdrawing from it.—*State v. Chavez,* 77 N.M. 274, 421 P.2d 796.

(9) Control of a narcotic substance is established by evidence that the narcotic was found in the premises occupied by the defendant.—*People v. Torres,* 5 Cal.App.2d 580, 43 P.2d 374; *People v. Oliver,* 66 Cal.App.2d 431, 152 P.2d 329; *People v. Harmon,* 89 Cal.App.2d 55, 200 P.2d 32; *People v. Brown,* 92 Cal.App.2d 360, 206 P.2d 1095; *People v. Robinson,* 110 Cal.App.2d 415, 242 P.2d 676 (found marijuana in toilet bowl); *People v. Hatton,* 114 Cal.-App.2d 195, 249 P.2d 901 (drugs fished out of wash basin); *People v. Stanciell,* 121 Cal.App.2d 798, 264 P.2d 576 (drugs in wall cabinet in defendant's bedroom).

(10) Narcotics found in the home occupied by the defendant raised a reasonable inference that they were his, even though he shared the home with others. "Without any statements about the ownership of the clothes or of the dresser, the jury could have concluded that the narcotics were in the possession of appellant" (*People v. Villaneueva,* 220 Cal.App.2d 443, 33 Cal.Rptr. 811; *People v. Elliott,* 186 Cal.App.2d 178, 8 Cal.Rptr. 795).—*People v. Ghimenti,* 42 Cal.Rptr. 504, 232 Cal.App.2d 76.

(11) Mere possession of a narcotic establishes a prima facie case and the lawfulness of the possession is a matter of defense.—*People v. Wallace,* 109 Cal.App.2d 676, 241 P.2d 264.

(12) When the evidence shows illegal possession of a narcotic by *someone* the corpus delicti of the crime of possession is established.—*People v. Bigelow,* 104 Cal.App.2d 380, 231 P.2d 881.

(13) To establish that the defendant had knowledge of the narcotic character of the substance he was charged with possessing (marijuana), the state is permitted to question him about details of his prior offense of possessing marijuana with intent to sell it.—*People v. Von Latta,* 65 Cal.Rptr. 651, 258 A.C.A. 417.

(14) The fact that the police did not keep the undercover agent under surveillance when he purchased the narcotics was not a gap in the proof necessary to establish the illegal sale.—*People v. Wolfe,* 70 Cal.Rptr. 86, 263 A.C.A. 923.

(15) The testimony of an officer that the defendant had numerous needle marks on his arm when arrested was admissible and material in defendant's trial for the possession of morphine because it characterized the intent with which it was possessed (morphine is injected).—*Brooks v. State,* 438 P.2d 25.

(16) Even though the accused may share his room with another, the finding of a narcotic substance in that room raises a reasonable inference that it is his.—*People v. Jones,* 65 Cal.Rptr. 878, 258 A.C.A. 751.

(17) There was sufficient proof that the defendant had knowledge of the narcotic nature of amphetamine tablets when it was shown that an officer inquired about getting some pills, was taken to the defendant's residence, and while there jargon relating to narcotics transactions was used and the officer was given some amphetamine tablets.—*People v. Jones,* 65 Cal.Rptr. 878, 258 A.C.A. 751.

(18) The fact that a defendant is under the influence of narcotics at the time he confessed (either self-administered or by police) does not, of itself, render that confession involuntary.—*Bryant v. State,* 229 Md. 531, 185 A.2d 190; *People v. Townsend,* 11 Ill.2d 30, 141 N.E.2d 729.

(19) A jury need not be instructed that the uncorroborated testimony of a police narcotics officer must be viewed with suspicion and acted on with caution or that such a rule is applicable to new recruits or novice officers.—*Bush v. United States,* 375 F.2d 602.

(20) The smell of distinctive odors could constitute evidence of a crime and of probable cause to make an arrest.—*Mullaney v. State,* 5 Md.App. 248, 246 A.2d 291.

(21) There is a fairly good discussion of the competency and reliability of narcotics addicts as witnesses in *State v. Booth,* 423 S.W.2d 820.

(22) The mere fact that the actual importation of the narcotics into the United States was done by an undercover narcotics agent did not absolve those initiating and participating in the crime from blame and did not preclude the proof of a corpus delicti of importation.—*Pederson v. United States,* 392 F.2d 41.

(23) The corpus delicti of the possession of marijuana may be proved circumstantially by an experienced narcotics officer testifying that the cigarette smoked by the defendant smelled and appeared to be marijuana (and the narcotic substance was never produced).—*People v. Marinos,* 67 Cal.Rptr. 452, 260 A.C.A. 779.

NEGLIGENCE

(1) "Gross negligence" is an "entire failure to exercise care or the exercise of so slight a degree of care as to justify a belief that there was an indifference to things and the welfare of others."—*People v. Madison,* 51 Cal.Rptr. 851, 242 Cal.App.2d 820.

(2) "Criminal negligence" consists of a measure of wantonness or flagrant or reckless disregard of the safety of others, or willful indifference to their safety.—*People v. Madison,* 51 Cal.Rptr. 851, 242 Cal.App.2d 820.

NEW TRIAL

(1) Perjury as ground for a new trial is discussed in 33 *A.L.R.* 550, 74 *A.L.R.* 757, 158 *A.L.R.* 1062.

(2) A motion for a new trial must be made and determined before a judgment is entered. Once a judgment has been entered, the trial court has no jurisdiction to hear such a motion.—*People v. Sainz,* 61 Cal.Rptr. 196, 253 Cal.App.2d 496.

OBSTRUCTING

(1) When an arrest is lawful the person arrested may not use passive resistance or interpose any obstacles which in any manner impede, hinder, interrupt, prevent or delay the arrest. A person who goes limp and requires the arresting officer to lift him bodily and carry him in order to make the arrest causes such delay and obstruction to the lawful arrest as to constitute the offense of "resisting an officer."—*In re Bacon,* 49 Cal.Rptr. 322, 240 Cal.-App.2d 34.

(2) "Obstructing" an officer is a felony that may be inherently dangerous to life calling for the application of the murder-felony rule.—*Brooks v. Superior Court of Los Angeles County,* 48 Cal.-Rptr. 762, 239 Cal.App.2d 538.

OPENING STATEMENT

(1) You need not prove what is stated in your opening statement unless it is done purposely to prejudice the defendant.—*Rutlege v. State,* 41 Ariz. 48, 15 P.2d 255; *Ragland v. State,* 404 P.2d 84.

(2) The state is not required to state a public offense in its opening statement. Opening statements do not put a limitation on the right of either party to introduce evidence.—*People v. Wilson,* 64 Cal.Rptr. 172, 256 Cal.App.2d 411.

(3) Where a codefendant had entered a guilty plea, the state could "lawfully expect" him to testify in conformity with his confession. Thus the state did not commit error in telling the jury that they expected codefendant to so testify. Also the fact that the codefendant's subsequent refusal thereafter to testify did not require a reversal (the witness claimed an invalid privilege under the Fifth).—*State v. Frazier,* 418 P.2d 841.

(4) Where the defense in their opening statement promise to prove something and they do not, the prosecution may comment upon such failure in its final argument.—*State v. McGonigle,* 103 Ariz. 267, 440 P.2d 100.

(5) Where the defendant's opening statement stated that his defense was entrapment and that issue was raised on the cross-examination of one of the state's witnesses, the state was permitted, in its case in chief, to offer evidence of the defendant's reputation for being a violator of liquor laws (with which he was charged).—*Porter v. United States,* 394 F.2d 508.

OPINION

(1) The feeling or mental attitude of people in frequent association may be given in the form of an opinion.—*State v. George,* 58 Wash. 681, 109 Pac. 114.

(2) The impeachment of a witness by medical testimony that the witness is a liar is discussed in 15 *A.L.R.* 932.

(3) An insanity expert may not give an opinion which is based in part on information coming to him from others.—175 *A.L.R.* 274.

(4) A doctor in arriving at his opinion on insanity may use materials gathered from psychological tests given by psychologists under his direction.—*State v. Coltharp,* 199 Kan. 598, 433 P.2d 418.

(5) An expert may express his opinion in terms of possibility, probability or actuality.—*Lester v. State,* 416 P.2d 52.

(6) An expert's testimony that hair samples were *probably* from decedent did not render his testimony inadmissible.—*State v. Harris,* 241 Ore. 224, 405 P.2d 492.

(7) An expert may testify to the facts upon which he bases his opinion even though these sources are inadmissible or inaccurate. —*People, Dept. of Public Works v. DiTomasco,* 57 Cal.Rptr. 293, 248 Cal.App.2d 741.

(8) A medical witness could give his opinion that a flashlight used as a club was a dangerous weapon.—*State v. Linville,* 127 Ore. 565, 273 Pac. 338.

(9) A director of a safety council who had been a sheriff for fourteen years and whose avocation was guns for thirty years could testify that the fatal arm wound could not have been inflicted by a bullet from the decedent's gun at close range.—*State v. Nelson,* 432 P.2d 857.

(10) A nonexpert investigating officer who had already testified to the skid marks found at the point of impact, the apparent automobile direction and the damage is permitted to indicate the position of the automobiles as they collided even though this is an opinion.—*Duran v. Mueller,* 79 Nev. 453, 386 P.2d 733.

(11) A witness other than a physician may—by training, study, and experience or special familiarity with the subject—be qualified to testify as to the cause of death (in discretion of the court). (Here a licensed embalmer, funeral director and special investigator gave his opinion on cause of death).—*Harvell v. State,* 395 P.2d 331.

(12) A physician's testimony as to the results of a blood test is admissible although he himself did not perform the blood test (his assistant did).—*State v. Boehme,* 71 Wash.2d 621, 430 P.2d 527.

(13) Where exemplars and the questioned writing are in evidence, a comparison may be made by the jury with or without the aid of the handwriting expert's testimony and the results of the comparisons are a matter for the jury.—*People v. Weiskopf,* 60 Cal.App.2d 214, 140 P.2d 201; *People v. Horowitz,* 70 Cal.-App.2d 675, 161 P.2d 833, 80 *A.L.R.2d* 272, 275, 276, 277.

(14) Anyone who is familiar with a person's handwriting from having seen him write is competent as a nonexpert witness to give his opinion on the genuineness of such person's signature.—*State v. Eubanks,* 86 Idaho 32, 383 P.2d 342.

(15) An autopsy surgeon may be permitted to testify to the murder victim's ability to talk after he had been wounded and the victim's perceptive powers after being wounded, even though the surgeon has never treated a person for a bullet wound.—*People v. Ketchel,* 30 Cal.Rptr. 538, 381 P.2d 394.

(16) An expert may give an opinion as to whether narcotics were possessed for sale by the defendant (after testifying as to his experience with the habits of users, quantities involved, the value of the narcotics found in defendant's possession and the customary method of packaging narcotics for use and sale).—*People v. Arguello,* 53 Cal.Rptr. 245, 244 Cal.App.2d 413.

(17) Testimony that the house where the killing occurred was in Ware County was not a "mere conclusion" and was admissible.—*Holmes v. State,* 224 Ga. 553, 163 S.E.2d 803.

(18) Allowing the pathologist who performed the autopsy on the victim of a vehicular manslaughter to answer a hypothetical question on the cause of the injuries was not error.—*State v. Wade,* 159 N.W.2d 396.

(19) The corpus delicti of the possession of marijuana may be proved circumstantially by an experienced narcotics officer testifying that the cigarette smoked by the defendant smelled and appeared to be marijuana (and the narcotic substance was never produced).—*People v. Marinos,* 67 Cal.Rptr. 452, 260 A.C.A. 779.

(20) The jury may disbelieve the testimony of a psychiatrist.—*People v. Scott,* 11 Mich.App. 576, 161 N.W.2d 753.

OTHER OFFENSES

(1) An officer's reference to the defendant's "past record" is not prejudicial error where the court admonishes the jury to disregard it.—*People v. DeLeon,* 67 Cal.Rptr. 45, 260 A.C.A. 155.

(2) On a charge of vehicular manslaughter (excessive speed), the state is allowed to cross-examine the defendant concerning his plea of guilty to traffic offense growing out of a similar incident to show his intent, knowledge and absence of mistake.—*State v. Roth,* 200 Kan. 677, 438 P.2d 58.

(3) Where the defense is that the defendant merely went to the scene of the robbery with another (who had confessed) and knew nothing about the planned robbery, the state may show that only recently the defendant had helped the other individual commit a different criminal offense.—*Hampton v. People,* 146 Colo. 570, 362 P.2d 864.

(4) When the defendant contended that he was drunk and could not have had the mental capacity to form the specific intent needed for burglary, the state could introduce evidence of defendant's prior burglary convictions to shed light on the defendant's intent, knowledge and plan.—*People v. Romero,* 53 Cal.-Rptr. 260, 244 Cal.App.2d 495.

(5) Evidence of a similar alleged burglary of another apartment by the defendants is relevant to rebut their claim of an innocent intent when they entered the apartment.—*People v. Rosenfield,* 52 Cal.Rpr. 101, 243 Cal.App.2d 60.

(6) The admission of an indecent exposure incident subsequent to the one charged was proper to show the intent, common scheme or plan (court must so limit in instructions) of the defendant.—*Wimple v. State,* 397 P.2d 696.

(7) Here an 18-year-old rape conviction was admitted as a similar offense. Age affects weight, not admissibility said the court.—*People v. Ing,* 55 Cal.Rptr. 902, 422 P.2d 590.

(8) In a charge of sale of narcotics where the defendant claimed entrapment, it is material to oppose that defense, that the defendant is a user of narcotics and that he had been previously involved in such a violation of the law.—*Notaro v. United States,* 363 F.2d 169.

(9) Under a possession of narcotics charge, it was admissible evidence that part of the narcotics the defendant was charged with possessing had been taken in a pharmacy burglary.—*People v. Rightnour,* 52 Cal.Rptr. 654, 243 Cal.App.2d 663.

(10) At least one case says that # 9 is true and admissible even though the state does not contend that the defendant committed the burglary.—*State v. Vindhurst,* 63 Wash.2d 607, 388 P.2d 552.

(11) Under a charge of beating a child to death, it is relevant to prove intent and to rebut the defendant's claim of accident to show that the defendant earlier had beaten other children.—*People v. York,* 51 Cal.Rptr. 661, 242 Cal.App.2d 560.

(12) The defendant assaulted his victim by pointing a gun at him and threatening him. The state showed (in its case in chief) that one week before the defendant and the victim (same one) met on a highway and the defendant pointed a gun at the victim. The court said this was admissible to show intent, lack of mistake or accident.—*State v. Kritzer,* 152 P.2d 967.

(13) In a prosecution for possession of heroin, it is proper for the state to prove, in its case in chief, prior sales of heroin by the defendant to show his guilty knowledge of the nature of the substance.—*Overton v. State,* 78 Nev. 198, 370 P.2d 677; *People v. Sogoian,* 42 Cal.Rptr. 736, 232 Cal.App.2d 430.

(14) To establish that the defendant had knowledge of the narcotic character of the substance he was charged with possessing (marijuana), the state is permitted to question him about details of his prior offense of possessing marijuana with intent to sell it.—*People v. Von Latta,* 65 Cal.Rptr. 651, 258 A.C.A. 417.

(15) The defendants armed themselves with knives and ice picks and assaulted a number of people. The court said that it was material to the issue of intent to show prior assaults shortly before the one in question, when done in the same manner.—*Adams v. State,* 191 S.E. 280.

(16) The admissibility of "other" fires in an arson case is discussed in 87 *A.L.R.2d* 891.

(17) The fact that a "similar offense" (to show common plan or design) occurred after the one charged, does not affect its admissibility.—*People v. Bartlett,* 64 Cal.Rptr. 503, 256 Cal.App.-2d 787.

(18) Evidence of a diagram of the floor plan of a cleaning plant found in the defendant's apartment when he was arrested for the robbery of a liquor store was admissible at his trial for the robbery and conspiracy involving the liquor store because it permitted a possible inference of a uniform plan of operation on the part of all defendants.—*People v. Collier,* 46 Cal.Rptr. 887, 237 Cal.App.2d 259.

(19) In a murder-felony case where rape was a material element, the state was permitted to show a prior rape because of its similarities to the one charged—in each case the defendant had a male companion with him, he had intercourse with the woman twice and he ripped off *all* of her clothing.—*People v. Whitehorn,* 60 C.2d 256, 383 P.2d 783.

(20) If evidence of "another offense" is admissible, it makes no difference that the defendant was acquitted of that other offense.—*People v. Griffin,* 32 Cal.Rptr. 24, 383 P.2d 432.

(21) In a prosecution for robbery and assault where the defendant hit the victim on the head with a hard object and stole her purse, the defendant's prior offenses of "purse snatching" and "rolling" victims were admissible to prove identity, scienter or guilty knowledge, intent, inclination or motive, plan, scheme or system of operation and to rebut the special defense.—*State v. Stephenson,* 191 Kan. 424, 381 P.2d 335.

(22) A "common plan" or "scheme" refers to some unique methodology or peculiar behavior pattern which tends to identify the perpetrator of the earlier crime as the person who perpetrated the crime charged and has no relevancy unless it aids in identifying the one who committed the act charged.—*People v. Baskett,* 47 Cal.Rptr. 274, 237 Cal.App.2d 712.

(23) The degree to which a "similar offense" must be proved is discussed in 3 *A.L.R.* 784.

(24) Where the defendant's testimony (charged with assault by means likely to produce great bodily injury) implied that she had been engaged in normal and reasonable handling of her patients in a rest home, the state could introduce other acts of violence to negate innocent intent.—*People v. Chambers,* 41 Cal.-Rptr. 551, 231 Cal.App.2d 23.

(25) The admissibility of evidence of "other offenses" to establish the identity of the defendant is discussed in 63 *A.L.R.* 602, 3 *A.L.R.* 1540, 22 *A.L.R.* 1016, 27 *A.L.R.* 357.

(26) It is not error for a witness in a prosecution for assault with a dangerous weapon to testify to the assault of someone other than the victim where it is impossible for the witness to describe the fight without alluding to the fact that several other persons were involved and perhaps injured.—*State v. Hale,* 432 P.2d 694.

(27) The fact that after the defendant struck the decedent he turned to a witness and said "You're next" was material to establish the defendant's aggressive state of mind when he struck the decedent.—*People v. Ogg,* 66 Cal.Rptr. 289, 258 Cal.App.2d 841.

(28) Proof of the "other crime" should be clear, beyond a reasonable doubt.—*Haley v. State,* 84 Tex.Cr.App. 629, 209 S.W. 675.

(29) Evidence, in an attempted abortion case, that one of the defendants was previously arrested for an illegal abortion and a description of the tools seized at that time was admissible to establish motive, intent, absence of mistake, common scheme or plan.—*Adams v. State,* 81 Nev. 524, 407 P.2d 169.

(30) The defendant and others rode around the city and assaulted one man at 9:30 P.M., two more at 10:30 P.M. and the victim at 11:00 P.M. The defendant said that he hit the victim in self-defense. Then the state put on the other victims and the court held such evidence admissible to rebut this claim of self-defense.—*Comm. v. Krolak,* 164 Pa.Super. 288, 64 A.2d 522.

(31) The defendant was charged with assault with intent to kill. He went into a saloon, got in a fist fight, left, came back with a butcher knife, the knife was taken away, and he went to his house and shortly thereafter shot the victim. The court said all of this was admissible to show the conduct and the state of mind and an intent to kill.—*State v. Clark,* 167 Pac. 84.

(32) The use of the defendant's parole officer as a witness against him was not an allusion to his prior record and was not error.—*People v. Saldivar,* 57 Cal.Rptr. 731, 249 Cal.App.2d 670.

PENETRATION

(1) Even though there is no rupture of the hymen and there are no lacerations, there may still be penetration enough for incest.—*Signs v. State,* 250 Pac. 938.

PERJURY

(1) False statements (under oath) in an application for a writ of habeas corpus constitute a basis for a change of perjury.—*People v. Pierce,* 52 Cal.Rptr. 853.

(2) You may have separate counts of perjury committed at the same hearing.—*Seymour v. United States,* 77 F.2d 577.

(3) The admission of parts of the official transcript of the prior trial was sufficient evidence to require submission of the issue as to whether the defendant, charged with perjury, had been sworn prior to that testimony, even though the official court reporter had no independent recollection of his being sworn.—*State v. Christenson,* 230 Ore. 283, 370 P.2d 240.

(4) Perjury as ground for new trial is discussed in 33 *A.L.R.* 550, 74 *A.L.R.* 757, 158 *A.L.R.* 1062.

PLEAS

(1) The defendant waives any irregularities in his preliminary examination when he pleads guilty in the district court or not guilty and goes to trial on the information.—*Cleveland v. State,* 199 Kan. 544, 407 P.2d 488.

(2) Evidence may not be admitted that one defendant (co-indictee or codefendant) has already pleaded or been found guilty.—48 *A.L.R.2d* 1016.

(3) "Plea bargaining" in which the defendant entered a plea of guilty to a forgery charge in exchange for the state's not filing similar charges and a habitual criminal charge did not constitute coercion which would require vacating and setting aside the sentence.—*Smith v. People,* 428 P.2d 69.

(4) The test for the validity of a guilty plea is whether the defendant understood the nature of the crime to which he pleaded and was able to weigh this understanding against his own knowledge of the act he had performed. Whether he knew of some degree of the crime to which he did not plead or its maximum sentence is irrelevant.—*Tucker v. Gladden,* 420 P.2d 625.

(5) When a defendant admits a "prior" he admits all the allegations of that "prior" contained in the information.—*People v. Ebner,* 49 Cal.Rptr. 690, 411 P.2d 578.

(6) A defendant's constitutional rights are not violated by allowing a codefendant to plead guilty to a lesser charge.—*Newman v. United States,* 382 F.2d 479.

(7) "Plea bargaining" with codefendants who testified against the defendant does not, ipso facto, constitute coerced testimony against the defendant.—*Minkin v. United States,* 383 F.2d 427.

(8) Defense counsel's advice to defendant that it would probably go easier with him if he pleaded guilty did not render the defendant's plea involuntary.—*State v. Tipton,* 78 N.M. 600, 435 P.2d 430.

(9) A plea of guilty is not coerced because the defendant was not advised by the court of his right to remain silent when called upon to plead.—*Hensley v. State,* 149 Kan. 728, 433 P.2d 344.

(10) A plea of guilty cannot be set aside merely because the defendant has a very low mentality. The only mental ability required to enter a valid guilty plea is a present ability to consult with an attorney and a reasonable degree of rational and factual understanding of the proceedings against him.—*Gantar v. Cox,* 74 N.M. 527, 395 P.2d 354.

(11) Codefendants may be punished differently for the same crime and the fact that one gets probation and the other does not, does not constitute cruel and unusual punishment.—*Bates v. State,* 436 P.2d 27.

(12) The coercion of a confession from a codefendant, who was to testify against the defendant, does not entitle the defendant to relief from his plea of guilty to murder on the ground that his plea was made under duress.—*Mullins v. Page,* 443 P.2d 773.

(13) A court need not advise the defendant of his right to the exclusion of illegally seized evidence prior to the proper acceptance of a guilty plea.—*State v. Cooper,* 161 N.W.2d 728.

(14) The mere offer to recommend a reduced sentence does not constitute a duressed guilty plea.—*People v. Bowman,* 40 Ill.-App. 116, 239 N.E.2d 433.

(15) Upon a guilty plea an involuntary confession is not admissible in a hearing to determine degree of guilt.—*United States ex rel. Sanders v. Maroney,* 397 F.2d 267.

(16) The fact that the accused was represented by able counsel at the time of his plea is a fact that argues against his claim that his plea was involuntary.—*State ex rel. Lawrence v. Henderson,* 433 S.W.2d 96.

(17) A plea of guilty is not rendered involuntary by the fact that it was partly induced by the possibility that a more serious charge might be prosecuted.—*Brewer v. Bennett,* 161 N.W.2d 749.

PRELIMINARY EXAMINATION

(1) The entire preliminary examination is waived by failing to move to quash the information.—*Ervin v. State,* 368 P.2d 256.

(2) "Jurisdiction" may be "lost" by failing to remand for a preliminary hearing when that fact is brought to the attention of the trial court.—*State v. Vaughn,* 74 N.M. 365, 393 P.2d 711.

(3) A defendant may consent and stipulate to being tried on the preliminary hearing transcript.—*People v. Morrison,* 65 Cal.-Rptr. 445, 258 A.C.A. 104.

(4) There was sufficient evidence for a finding of probable cause at a preliminary hearing on a burglary charge when it was shown that the defendant was found in a damaged store in a riot area (Watts).—*Reed v. Superior Court,* 47 Cal.Rptr. 815, 238 Cal.App.2d 321.

(5) Upon receiving a magistrate's order holding for trial, the reviewing court will not delve into the magistrate's decisions on the credence of witnesses, the weight of the evidence or the resolving of conflicts in the evidence.—*People v. Pierce,* 52 Cal.Rptr. 853; *People v. Sullivan,* 51 Cal.Rptr. 778, 242 Cal.App.2d 767; *People v. Brice,* 44 Cal.Rptr. 231, 234 Cal.App.2d 258.

(6) A defendant who pleads not guilty before moving to set aside the information is not entitled to a reversal of his conviction because of the introduction of certain evidence at his preliminary examination.—*People v. Wester,* 46 Cal.Rptr. 699, 237 Cal.App.2d 232.

(7) A confession by itself is enough to establish probable cause. —*United States v. Kallas,* 272 Fed. 742; *Application of Berry,* 43 Cal.2d 838, 279 P.2d 18; *Lambus v. Kaiser,* 352 Mo. 122, 176 S.W.2d 494; *People ex rel. Odell v. Holl,* 124 N.Y.S.2d 289; *United States v. Bloomgarten,* Fed.Cas. No. 14, 612; *United States v. Burr,* Fed.Cas. No. 14, 692 A.

(8) Where a magistrate refused to let the defendant call witnesses at his preliminary examination, the trial court has a duty to remand the case for a full preliminary examination.—*State ex rel. Hanagan v. Armijo,* 72 N.M. 50, 380 P.2d 196.

(9) A preliminary examination is not a "trial" and the complaint and warrant used there are not to be construed with the strictness of papers filed in the trial court (such as an information).—*State v. Earley,* 192 Kan. 167, 386 P.2d 189.

(10) The lack of probable cause at a preliminary examination cannot be raised by a motion to quash—it must be done by habeas corpus.—*People v. Dal Porto,* 17 Cal.App.2d 755, 62 P.2d 1061; *People v. Dal Porto,* 17 Cal.App.2d 755, 63 P.2d 1199.

(11) A defendant may constitutionally waive a preliminary examination without the aid of counsel.—*State v. Crowe,* 190 Kan. 658, 378 P.2d 89.

(12) The failure to appoint counsel at a preliminary examination is not error.—*White v. Crouse,* 193 Kan. 674, 396 P.2d 333; *Sanders v. Cox,* 74 N.M. 525, 395 P.2d 353.

(13) The test applied to sustain a magistrate's ruling binding the defendant over for trial is discussed in *State v. Kubiak,* 257 Wis. 159, 42 N.W.2d 496.

(14) In determining whether "probable cause" exists where the evidence is conflicting and different inferences may reasonably be drawn, the conclusion of the magistrate *must* prevail over the conclusion of the trial judge, who saw only the transcripts of the prelim exam.—*People v. Beasley,* 250 Cal.App.2d 71, 58 Cal.Rptr. 485.

(15) "On appeal from the judgment of a district court in a habeas corpus proceeding, it is not the province of this court to review errors claimed, by one of the parties, to have been committed by a magistrate in the course of a preliminary examination."—*Kelly v. Kurtz,* 183 Kan. 684, 331 P.2d 327.

(16) There is no requirement that a magistrate in conducting a preliminary exam stick as strictly to the rules of evidence and procedure as a trial judge at trial.—*State v. Earley,* 192 Kan. 167, 386 P.2d 189.

(17) Where it is shown to a trial court that the defendant has been denied a constitutional right at his preliminary examination, the trial court must abate the information until there has been a proper preliminary examination, remand the accused to the magistrate for such an examination; and the trial court does not lose jurisdiction of the information and the filing of a new information (after the defendant is once again held for trial) is not required. —*State v. Vaughn,* 74 N.M. 365, 393 P.2d 711.

(18) The dismissal of a charge by a magistrate at a preliminary examination is not res judicata and a second charge may be filed. —*People v. Joseph,* 153 Cal.App.2d 548, 314 P.2d 1004.

(19) A good discussion of the power and correctness of the state filing a second complaint after the defendant has been discharged at a preliminary examination takes place in *Tell v. Wolke,* 21 Wis.2d 613, 124 N.W.2d 655.

(20) A discharge upon habeas corpus for failure of proof does not bar further prosecution upon another indictment for the same offense.—*In re Begerow,* 136 Cal. 393, 68 Pac. 773, 56 *L.R.A.* 528.

(21) The state is not required to produce all of its evidence at a preliminary examination but only enough to satify the magistrate of probable cause.—*Carey v. State,* 91 Idaho 706, 429 P.2d 836.

(22) Where the mental competency of the defendant is before a magistrate at or prior to the preliminary examination, the magistrate should bind the defendant over and the competency issue should be determined in the trial court after a determination by the trial court that there was probable cause.—*State v. McCredden,* 33 Wis.2d 661, 148 N.W.2d 33.

(23) Even though the state's witnesses testified at the preliminary examination that the burglary occurred on August 8, a court need not grant the defendant another preliminary examination when it is shown that the burglary really took place on September 8.—*State v. Robertson,* 190 Kan. 771, 378 P.2d 37.

(24) Even if there was undue delay between the defendant's arrest and his appearance before the justice of the peace, this did not deprive the justice of jurisdiction to bind the defendant over for trial.—*State v. Elledge,* 78 N.M. 157, 429 P.2d 355.

(25) Admission of an absent witness' preliminary examination testimony is valid even though at the preliminary examination the witness had not been fully or adequately cross-examined.—*People v. Berger,* 66 Cal.Rptr. 213, 258 Cal.App.2d 622.

(26) A coroner's warrant, after a coroner's jury verdict, takes the place of a complaint and is sufficient authority for holding a preliminary hearing before the magistrate.—*Uhock v. Hand,* 182 Kan. 419, 320 P.2d 794; *State v. Denevan,* 49 S.D. 192, 206 N.W. 927; *State v. Brecount,* 82 Kan. 195, 107 Pac. 763; *State v. Tennison,* 39 Kan. 726, 18 Pac. 948; *Hogg v. Whitham,* 120 Kan. 341, 242 Pac. 1021.

(27) The defendant waives any irregularities in his preliminary examination when he pleads guilty in district court or not guilty and goes to trial on the information.—*Cleveland v. State,* 195 Kan. 544, 407 P.2d 488.

(28) A magistrate's statement to the defendant at a preliminary hearing that he may or may not testify but if he does, anything he says may be used against him, did not judicially intimidate the defendant and thus render his statements inadmissible.—*Wright v. State,* 199 Kan. 136, 427 P.2d 611.

(29) The defendant did not have a right to court-appointed counsel at a preliminary hearing where he was identified by the victim of the robbery.—*Tyler v. State,* 5 Md.App. 265, 246 A.2d 634.

(30) A dismissal of a charge by a magistrate at the preliminary examination stage because he determined the evidence was illegally seized does not preclude the refiling of the identical charge by indictment.—*People v. Prewitt,* 52 Cal.2d 330, 341 P.2d 1.

PREMEDITATION

(1) The number of shots may show premeditation and deliberation.—*State v. Cunningham,* 144 P.2d 303.

(2) A "presumption" of premeditation arises from a killing with a deadly weapon.—*State v. Lartenschlager,* 22 Minn. 514; *State v. Prolow,* 98 Minn. 459, 108 N.W. 873; *State v. Brown,* 41 Minn. 319, 43 N.W. 69; *State v. Lentz,* 45 Minn. 177, 47 N.W. 720; *Hogan v. State,* 36 Wis. 226; *Copps v. State,* 120 Wis. 504, 97 N.W. 210.

PRIOR CONVICTIONS

(1) An instruction telling the jury their function in regard to the "habitual criminal statute" and the posture of the case when that point has been reached is not a comment on the evidence.—*State v. Bryant,* 437 P.2d 398.

(2) There is no fatal variance in charging a "prior" on the date when the verdict (or the plea) was returned and proving the date of the prior as the date when the sentence was imposed.—*State v. Silva,* 78 N.M. 286, 430 P.2d 783; *In re Williams,* 257 A.C.A. 686, 65 Cal.Rptr. 52.

(3) Where a photograph was part of an exhibit of authenticated copies of a prior, the typewritten information on the back of the photo showing when the defendant was received and discharged at the prison was admissible to establish the defendant's presence at the prison between those dates.—*People v. Caruth,* 47 Cal.-Rptr. 29, 237 Cal.App.2d 401.

(4) A "prior" must precede the commission of the offense charged in order to enhance the punishment.—*State v. Felton,* 194 Kan. 501, 399 P.2d 817.

(5) When a defendant admits a "prior" he admits all the allegations of that "prior" contained in the information.—*People v. Ebner,* 49 Cal.Rptr. 690, 411 P.2d 578.

(6) The Original Document Rule is not applicable in a habitual offender proceeding where the exhibits were offered to prove identity and they were original records kept by the sheriff concerning the commitment of persons to his custody.—*State v. Silva,* 78 N.M. 286, 430 P.2d 783.

(7) Where one of the defendant's "priors" was a burglary, punishable *only* by imprisonment in the state prison, but he nevertheless was sent to the county jail, that invalid sentence did not convert the crime into a misdemeanor and it could still be used as a felony "prior."—*State v. Commedore,* 239 Ore. 82, 396 P.2d 216.

(8) In determining whether an out-of-state "prior" is a felony in your state, the controlling date (as to statutory amendments) is the date of that "prior"—you don't make the determination as of "now" but as of "then."—*State v. Lott,* 73 N.M. 280, 387 P.2d 855.

(9) Where a "prior" is an essential element of the crime presently charged, it is referred to in the pleading, is read to the jury, must be proved and may be mentioned in argument.—*People v. Shaw,* 46 Cal.Rptr. 217.

(10) In a prosecution for petty theft with a "prior" of petty theft, the defendant is entitled to confess to the "prior" outside the presence of the jury and eliminate it as an issue; then disclosure of that "prior" to the jury is reversible error.—*People v. Cooks,* 44 Cal.Rptr. 819, 235 Cal.App. 226.

(11) Where a prior conviction (charged) makes the offense a felony, the offense charged does not become a misdemeanor when the prior conviction is admitted, and the defendant is still subject to imprisonment as a felon and the offense is cognizable in superior court (the trial court).—*People v. Shaw,* 46 Cal.Rptr. 217.

(12) The introduction into evidence of authenticated and certified copies of the judgment, sentence, photographs and fingerprints of the defendant's prior conviction did not deny the defendant due process or a constitutional right of confrontation.—*Richardson v. State,* 432 S.W.2d 100.

(13) The mere fact that during his testimony a police officer tells the jury that he knew the defendant before he apprehended him does not indicate to the jury that the defendant has had prior trouble with the police.—*State v. Knicker,* 424 S.W.2d 605.

(14) The prosecution is not required to inform the defendant, prior to trial, of the criminal record of the state's witnesses.—*Hemphill v. United States,* 392 F.2d 45.

(15) The defendant was not twice put in jeopardy when the prosecution used his 1960 conviction to increase the penalty on his current conviction.—*Anderson v. Wilson,* 397 F.2d 255.

(16) The fact that the prosecuting authorities utilized the Habitual Offender statute only when the prior conviction was within their state did not give rise to a claim of a denial of equal protection.—*State v. Baldonado,* 79 N.M. 175, 441 P.2d 215.

PRISONS

(1) A prisoner has no right of privacy in his jail cell except to consult with his attorney in a room set aside for that purpose.—*People v. Lopez,* 32 Cal.Rptr. 424, 84 P.2d 16.

(2) The personal effects of an arrestee may be removed and examined to see if they are stolen property. They may be returned to him upon his release or preserved for use as evidence at trial.—*People v. Ross,* 60 Cal.Rptr. 254, 429 P.2d 606.

PRIVILEGES

(1) In a prosecution of a husband for attempted murder, the wife's claim of the physician-patient privilege was properly overruled as to information gained by the physicians who treated her after her husband tried to kill her because the evidence would cause little additional embarrassment and would not subject her to any criminal liability.—*State v. Boehme,* 430 P.2d 527.

(2) The testimony of a doctor is admissible where the doctor is *not* consulted for treatment.—107 *A.L.R.* 1495.

(3) Where a doctor was sent by the district attorney *solely* for the purpose of examining the accused in order to report upon his sanity, the relation of physician and patient did not exist between the doctor and the accused.—*State v. Fouquette,* 67 Nev. 505, 221 P.2d 404.

(4) The physician-patient privilege is destroyed by the presence of a nurse.—*Southwest Metals Co. v. Gomez,* 4 F.2d 215.

(5) The physician-patient privilege cannot be assumed from a "clinic" association.—*Hawkins v. Thornton,* 92 Ariz. 211, 375 P.2d 565.

(6) Symptoms of the intoxicated condition of the defendant observed by a doctor are not communications which are necessary for the physician to prescribe relief and thus are admissible. —*State v. Townsend,* 146 Kan. 982, 73 P.2d 1124; *Perry v. Hannagan,* 257 Mich. 120, 241 N.W. 233; *State v. Aguirre,* 167 Kan. 266, 206 P.2d 118; *City of Racine v. Woitechek,* 251 Wis. 404, 29 N.W.2d 752.

(7) The taking of blood is not necessary to enable a physician to prescribe relief or remedy and thus the blood is not "privileged."—*Hanlon v. Woodhouse,* 113 Colo. 504, 160 P.2d 998; *Wolf v. People,* 187 P.2d 926; *People v. Downs,* 5 App.Div.2d 935, 172 N.Y.S.2d 377; *Schwartz v. Schneuringer,* 269 Wis. 535, 69 N.W.2d 756. Contra: *Alder v. State,* 239 Ind. 68, 154 N.E.2d 716.

(8) A compulsory mental examination of a defendant does not violate his privilege against self-incrimination.—*Holt v. United States,* 218 U.S. 245, 54 L.Ed. 1021, Wigmore, 3rd ed. § 2263, § 2265, 28 *J. Crim. C & Crim.* 261, 59 Har.L.R. 481, 521-523, 25 *A.L.R.2d* 1407; *United States v. Hohn,* 198 F.2d 934; *State v. Nelson,* 162 Ore. 430, 92 P.2d 182.

(9) Where a psychiatrist interviewed the defendant at the request of the state, the psychiatrist was an agent of the state with no more right than any such agent to elicit admissions from the defendant without his being informed of his rights and his admissions of guilt to the psychiatrist should be excluded.—*People v. Polk,* 44 Cal.Rptr. 773, 402 P.2d 845.

(10) If a husband and wife conspire together, they cannot claim immunity from prosecution on the basis of their marital status.—*People v. Pierce,* 40 Cal.Rptr. 845, 395 P.2d 893.

(11) A defendant who objects to his "wife" testifying against him has burden of proving that she is married to him.—*State v. Clyde,* 47 Hawaii 345, 388 P.2d 846.

(12) A crime against the child of a spouse is a crime against the spouse.—*Balltrip v. People,* 157 Colo. 108, 401 P.2d 259, 82 *A.L.R.* 644.

(13) A wife could properly consent to the taking of two of her husband's (defendant) suits from their trailer.—*United States v. Alloway,* 397 F.2d 105.

(14) In some cases the state may comment on the failure of the defendant to produce his wife as a witness.—*Ferrell v. State,* 429 S.W.2d 901.

(15) The physician-patient privilege does not apply to the testimony of a physician who examined the defendant for the purpose of commitment.—*People v. Lipscomb,* 263 A.C.A. 61, 69 Cal.Rptr. 127.

(16) A physician, suspecting his patient of nothing criminal, was not required to give the patient the *Miranda* warnings before, during or after the examination.—*Edwards v. State,* 244 Ark. 1145, 429 S.W.2d 92.

PROBATION

(1) There is neither a constitutional nor a statutory right to notice and a hearing preceding the revocation of probation.—*People v. Daugherty,* 43 Cal.Rptr. 446, 233 Cal.App.2d 284.

(2) "Probation is a favor."—*People v. McCann,* 43 Cal.Rptr. 789, 233 Cal.App.2d 561.

(3) To revoke probation it is not necessary that the breach of conditions be proved beyond a reasonable doubt; it is sufficient if the proof is clear and satisfactory and convinces the court.—*State v. Nelson,* 196 Kan. 592, 412 P.2d 1018.

(4) Where the defendant was given probation on condition he spend the first ten months in the county jail, the condition did not render the crime a misdemeanor.—*People v. Esparza,* 61 Cal.-Rptr. 167, 253 Cal.App.2d 362.

PROHIBITION

(1) Prohibition may not be used to stay a criminal trial.—*Shelby v. Sixth Judicial District Ct.,* 82 Nev. 204, 414 P.2d 942.

(2) In habeas corpus, prohibition or certiorari proceedings, "jurisdiction" is not limited to its fundamental meaning, and judicial acts may be restrained or annulled if it is determined that they are in excess of a court's powers as defined by the constitution, a statute or court rules.—*In re Zerbe,* 36 Cal.Rptr. 286, 388 P.2d 182.

PROSECUTION

(1) Any person may file a criminal complaint, not just the county attorney.—*Scott v. Justice's Court of Tahoe Tp.*, 435 P.2d 747.

(2) A defendant may not have the charges against him dismissed simply because he was not brought before a magistrate within a reasonable time after arrest.—*Gottfried v. People,* 158 Colo. 510, 408 P.2d 431.

(3) The dismissal of a complaint in justice court does not bar a subsequent prosecution in superior court for the same offense.—*State v. Weiss,* 438 P.2d 610.

(4) The fact that some wrongdoers are prosecuted and others are not does not amount to illegal discrimination.—*People v. Maldonado,* 50 Cal.Rptr. 45, 240 Cal.App.2d 812.

(5) There is nothing unconstitutional in the government having a choice as to what crime it will prosecute when the facts give a choice.—*Minkin v. United States,* 383 F.2d 427.

(6) The defendant may not claim prejudice because a witness against him has been granted immunity from any crime growing out of the transactions about which he was being questioned.—*State v. Dickens,* 66 Wash.2d 58, 401 P.2d 321.

(7) "Due process does not require that the state establish guilt beyond a reasonable doubt."—*United States ex rel. Morton v. Mancusi,* 393 F.2d 482.

(8) The state is bound by its promise to dismiss the prosecution if the defendant passes a lie-detector test.—*Florida v. Davis,* 188 So.2d 24.

(9) The state's investigative duties do not end with the preliminary examination. They may, at any time, seek to know what a witness may testify to at trial.—*State v. Jones,* 202 Kan. 31, 446 P.2d 851.

(10) The victim's granting of time to the defendant to pay off the bad check does not insulate the defendant from criminal liability.—*State v. Burton,* 8 Ariz.App. 186, 444 P.2d 743.

(11) A plea of guilty is not rendered involuntary by the fact that it was partly induced by the possibility that a more serious charge might be prosecuted.—*Brewer v. Bennett,* 161 N.W.2d 749.

(12) The fact that the prosecuting authorities utilized the Habitual Offender statute only when the prior conviction was within their state did not give rise to a denial of equal protection.—*State v. Baldonado,* 79 N.M. 175, 441 P.2d 215.

(13) An illegal arrest, search and seizure does not grant one immunity from prosecution.—*People v. Moore,* 72 Cal.Rptr. 800, 446 P.2d 800.

PUBLIC OFFICERS

(1) Public officers are assumed to have performed their statutory duties, in the absence of an allegation to the contrary.—*Petition of Jones,* 143 Mont. 19, 386 P.2d 747.

PUBLIC PLACE

(1) The defendant urinated in the yard of the house which he occupied with the complainant (one half each) and the act took place where the defendant could have exposed himself to the windows of other dwelling houses. The court said that the place is public if the exposure is such that it is likely to be seen by a number of casual observers. It is sufficient if the place is not ordinarily public, but only in consequence of persons being temporarily assembled there. There is no need that the exposure should be actually seen by any one, provided that it was made to be seen and those who were there could have seen it if they had looked and it is immaterial whether the exposure was made to one person or to many.—*Van Houten v. State,* 46 N.J.L. 16, 50 Am.-Rep. 397.

(2) The defendant was in a "public place" in his car alongside the curb (lawfully parked) with the ignition off.—*People v. Belanger,* 53 Cal.Rptr. 660, 243 Cal.App.2d 654.

(3) When hit-and-run statute is silent as to where the offense must occur, it is not necessary to allege or prove that the offense occurred on a public highway.—*People v. Stansberry,* 51 Cal.-Rptr. 403, 242 Cal.App.2d 199.

PUNISHMENT

(1) Codefendants may be punished differently for the same crime and the fact that one gets probation and the other does not does not constitute cruel and unusual punishment.—*Bates v. State,* 436 P.2d 27.

RAP SHEETS

(1) Rap sheets from the F.B.I. are pure hearsay.—*State v. Taylor,* 198 Kan. 290, 424 P.2d 612.

RAPE

(1) Where two or more people at the same time and place and as part of a common design rape a woman, there is a continuing act of rape and the acts of the codefendants are admissible as part of the *res gestae.*—*Brown v. State,* 435 P.2d 173.

(2) Rape by fraud or impersonation is discussed in 91 *A.L.R.2d* 591.

(3) A charge of assault with intent to commit rape includes the crime of attempt to rape.—*State v. Hall,* 88 Idaho 177, 397 P.2d 261.

(4) In a sex case it may be permissible to introduce pyschiatric testimony concerning the mental and emotional condition of the "victim."—*Ballard v. Superior Court of San Diego County,* 49 Cal.Rptr. 302, 401 P.2d 838.

(5) In an assault with intent to commit rape, there is enough evidence to support a finding of a specific intent to have intercourse by force when it is shown that the defendant entered the victim's bedroom masked, climbed on the bed, straddled her and began to stroke her neck when she awoke. (His pants were not unzippered and she had a sheet over her body the whole time.) —*State v. Kekaualua,* 50 Hawaii 138, 433 P.2d 131.

(6) The prosectrix in a rape case need not make a direct statement that she was not married to the defendant.—*People v. Harrell,* 60 Cal.Rptr. 864, 252 Cal.App.2d 735.

(7) The fact that the rape victim, who was 15, had, prior to the act, been married is not a defense to statutory rape.—*People v. Caldwell,* 63 Cal.Rptr. 63, 255 Cal.App.2d 299.

REASONABLE DOUBT

(1) It is error for a trial court to give an instruction attempting to define reasonable doubt.—*Wilson v. State,* 403 P.2d 262.

(2) "The doctrine of reasonable doubt applies to proof of guilt and not to the establishment of each incident or event inculpating the defendant."—*People v. Klinkenberg,* 90 Cal.App.2d 608, 204 P.2d 47; *People v. Kross,* 112 Cal.App.2d 602. 247 P.2d 44.

(3) Due process does not require that the state establish guilt beyond a reasonable doubt.—*United States ex rel. Morton v. Mancusi,* 393 F.2d 482.

REBUTTAL

(1) Where a defendant testified and left the impression that a deputy sheriff had stated that the defendant was not drunk at the time in question, it was proper to put that deputy sheriff on the stand in rebuttal to state that he made no such statement even though this testimony might properly have been presented in the state's case in chief.—*Dickerson v. State,* 422 P.2d 213; *Henderson v. State,* 64 Cal.Rptr. 494, 389 P.2d 363.

(2) "Rebuttal evidence" is evidence which is presented in denial of some fact which the adverse party has attempted to prove in his case.—*State v. Freeman,* 195 Kan. 561, 408 P.2d 612.

(3) A witness may be called in rebuttal who has not been endorsed on the information.—*Dickerson v. State,* 422 P.2d 213.

RECENTLY STOLEN PROPERTY

(1) Possession of recently stolen property is a circumstance which may be considered with all other facts in determining the guilt of a defendant charged with receiving stolen property.—*State v. Tollett,* 71 Wash.2d 806, 431 P.2d 168.

(2) Recent and unexplained possession of the fruits of a robbery is a very incriminating circumstance and may, coupled with other facts, be sufficient to support a conviction for robbery.—*Martinez v. People,* 156 Colo. 380, 399 P.2d 415.

(3) After showing that the defendant was in possession of recently stolen property, little more is needed to sustain a conviction for receiving stolen property.—*People v. Beasley,* 58 Cal.-Rptr. 485, 250 Cal.App.2d 71.

(4) Joint possession with another of a garage where stolen property was found would sustain a conviction for receiving that property.—*People v. Lees,* 64 Cal.Rptr. 888, 257 Cal.App.2d 363.

(5) In order to prove a charge of "receiving stolen property," it is not necessary to first prove that the defendant is not the thief who stole the property.—*People v. Hansard,* 53 Cal.Rptr. 918, 245 Cal.App.2d 691; *People v. Marquez,* 47 Cal.Rptr. 166.

(6) "In a prosecution for receiving stolen goods, the defendant cannot offer in evidence the judgment acquitting the thief as that is *res inter alias acta.*"—*State v. Phillips,* 24 Mo. 475; *State v. Ross,* 29 Mo. 32; *Comm'th v. Williams,* 3 Gray (Mass.) 461; *State v. Sweeten,* 75 Mo.App. 127.

(7) A charge of receiving need not allege the name of the person from whom the defendant received the property.—*Wertheimer v. State,* 201 Ind. 572, 169 N.E. 40, 68 *A.L.R.* 178.

(8) The defendant's possession of recently stolen property may be proved by either direct or circumstantial evidence.—*State v. Collins,* 435 P.2d 538.

(9) The rule requiring a defendant to explain his possession of recently stolen property or have his failure used against him does not compel him to "take the stand" in violation of the Fifth Amendment.—*People v. DeLeon,* 46 Cal.Rptr. 241, 236 Cal.App.-2d 530. See *Pugh v. State,* 416 P.2d 637. And an instruction to this effect (defendant's failure to explain possession) is not improper; *People v. DeLeon,* 46 Cal.Rptr. 241, 236 Cal.App.2d 530. Apparently contra: *Payne v. State,* 435 P.2d 424.

(10) Property is "recently stolen" when found three days after the theft.— *State v. Jenkins,* 197 Kan. 651, 421 P.2d 33.

(11) Three weeks is "recent."—*Jones v. State,* 5 Md.App. 180, 245 A.2d 897.

(12) Property is "recently stolen" even after a 39-day period.—*State v. Ledbetter,* 17 Utah 2d 353, 412 P.2d 312.

(13) Possession of stolen property plus a lousy explanation or suspicious circumstances permits an inference that the property was received with knowledge that it was stolen. A "suspicious circumstance" is an alteration of the property to prevent identification; so is a horribly low price "paid" for the property.—*People v. Brumley,* 51 Cal.Rptr. 131, 242 Cal.App.2d 124.

(14) A fictitious name is also a suspicious circumstance.—*State v. Tollett,* 71 Wash.2d 806, 431 P.2d 168.

(15) The possession of recently stolen goods as evidence of guilty knowledge is discussed in 68 *A.L.R.* 187.

RECORDINGS

(1) A recording of defendant's statements to an officer after being warned of his right to counsel and to remain silent is admissible.—*People v. Escobedo,* 58 Cal.Rptr. 426, 250 Cal.App.2d 417.

(2) Recording a defendant's confession without warning him that it is being recorded does not render the statement inadmissible.—*People v. Lewis,* 53 Cal.Rptr. 108, 244 Cal.App.2d 325; *Lee v. Wilson,* 363 F.2d 824; *United States v. Knohl,* 379 F.2d 427.

(3) Secretly recorded statements of defendant to a codefendant in jail may be admitted without violating the defendant's constitutional rights.—*People v. Boulad,* 45 Cal.Rptr. 104, 235 Cal.-App.2d 118.

(4) Statements to an informant on a concealed tape are admissible.—*Hurst v. United States,* 370 F.2d 161.

(5) An officer may testify to conversations he heard over a receiver concealed on an informer's person.—*United States v. Jackson,* 390 F.2d 317; *Handsferd v. United States,* 390 F.2d 373.

(6) The use of a transmitter and a recording device concealed on a confederate, who has agreed to cooperate in obtaining statements from the defendant do not violate the United States Constitution (4th, 5th or 6th).—*Garrett v. United States,* 382 F.2d 768.

(7) The deletion of inaudible, irrelevant or repetitive portions of a tape recording does not render it inadmissible.—*United States v. Maxwell,* 383 F.2d 437.

(8) Although portions of a tape recording are inaudible, the tape is admissible if the import of the conversation is conveyed. —*United States v. Cooper,* 365 F.2d 246.

(9) The admissibility of sound recordings in evidence is discussed in 58 *A.L.R.2d* 1024.

(10) Testimony that a tape recording fairly and accurately reproduced the interrogation and that one could hear and understand the contents of the tape was an adequate foundation to establish the accuracy of the recording.—*People v. Spencer,* 31 Cal.Rptr. 782, 383 P.2d 134.

(11) An authentic and accurate re-recording is admissible after a proper foundation is laid over an objection that it is not the best evidence.—*United States v. Knohl,* 379 F.2d 427.

RECORDS

(1) One of the records required to be kept by law, a motor-vehicle registration "stub," was competent and the best evidence of the ownership of the auto stolen.—*Raullerson v. People,* 159 Colo. 395, 412 P.2d 236.

(2) It is proper to admit hospital records consisting of nurses' notes in an automobile accident case resulting in the subsequent death of a passenger.—*Plank v. Heirigs,* 156 N.W.2d 193.

(3) Permitting federal agents to testify that the records of the Department of the Interior showed no application of the defendant for permission to possess more than the statutory limit of mourning doves was not error as against an objection based upon the Best Evidence Rule.—*Aiuppa v. United States,* 393 F.2d 597.

REFRESHING RECOLLECTION

(1) A discussion of "refreshing the recollection of a witness" by memos or other writings appears in 125 *A.L.R.* 19.

(2) The use of memos or writings to refresh a witness' memory does not make that memo admissible.—*Lewis v. Schaffer,* 369 P.2d 639.

(3) If only part of a document is used to refresh a recollection, other parts of the document which are relevant to the part already known to the judge and jury are admissible.—*Gallegos v. People,* 157 Colo. 484, 403 P.2d 864.

(4) Where a witness uses any paper to refresh his memory while he is on the witness stand, the opposing side, on proper demand, may examine the paper and use it on cross-examination. —*Jackson v. United States,* 250 F.2d 897.

(5) An officer may refresh his recollection from an unsigned statement of a defendant whose questions and answers the officer had typed.—*Miller v. Statev,* 251 Md. 362, 247 A.2d 530.

REPUTATION

(1) How does remoteness affect the admissibility of evidence of the defendant's good reputation? It is discussed in 87 *A.L.R.2d* 968.

(2) Negative proof of good character or reputation of the defendant is discussed in 67 *A.L.R.* 1210.

(3) A witness testifying to the good character or reputation of a defendant in a criminal prosecution may be interrogated on cross-examination with respect to rumors or reports of particular acts imputed to the defendant and as to what the witness has heard of specific charges of misconduct made against the defendant.—71 *A.L.R.* 1504.

(4) Where the defendant's expert insanity witness testified that the defendant was "characteristically a passive man," the state

was allowed to show the defendant's reputation in the community for being quarrelsome.—*State v. Johnson,* 69 Wash.2d 264, 418 P.2d 238.

(5) Where the defendant's opening statement stated that his defense was entrapment and that issue was raised on the cross-examination of one of the state's witnesses the state was permitted, in its case in chief, to offer evidence of the defendant's reputation for being a violator of liquor laws (with which he was charged).—*Porter v. United States,* 394 F.2d 508.

RES JUDICATA

(1) *Res judicata* in criminal cases is discussed in 147 *A.L.R.* 992.

(2) The dismissal of a charge at a preliminary examination is not *res judicata* and a second charge may be filed.—*People v. Joseph,* 153 Cal.App.2d 548, 314 P.2d 1004. Also *People v. Prewitt,* 52 Cal.2d 330, 341 P.2d 1.

(3) A reversal on appeal is not a bar to a retrial of the reversed case (against an argument of double jeopardy).—*State v. Bloomer,* 197 Kan. 668, 421 P.2d 58.

(4) Dismissal of a felony prosecution (before jeopardy had attached) is not a bar to filing a new action on the same charge.—*People v. Hernandez,* 58 Cal.Rptr. 835, 250 Cal.App.2d 842.

(5) A magistrate's determination of a search and seizure question is not *res judicata.*—*People v. Prewitt,* 52 Cal.2d 330, 341 P.2d 1.

(6) The defendant who was convicted of violating a city ordinance prohibiting the carrying of a concealed weapon was not placed in double jeopardy when he was subsequently convicted in a county court under a statute prohibiting certain convicted felons from carrying pistols as a result of the same incident.—*Earwood v. State,* 198 Kan. 659, 426 P.2d 151.

(7) A defendant who pleaded guilty to a charge of driving an automobile without having his operator's license in his immediate possession when he knew he was not guilty, for the express purpose of immunizing himself against further prosecution for the more serious offense of driving at a time when his operator's license had been revoked procured his "conviction" and foreclosed himself from urging double jeopardy.—*Hampton v. Municipal Court of Pasadena Judicial Dist., Los Angeles County,* 51 Cal.Rptr. 760, 242 Cal.App.2d 689.

(8) An acquittal on a charge of transporting narcotics does not prohibit a prosecution for the possession of the narcotics allegedly transported.—*People v. Webb,* 52 Cal.Rptr. 495.

(9) In determining whether the defendant can successfully plead double jeopardy, the trial court may look to the entire record of the former trial and is not restricted to the indictment or information alone.—*Price v. State,* 437 P.2d 330.

(10) A defendant may be prosecuted for driving while intoxicated in district court after the state has entered a nolle prosequi in justice court.—*State v. Sweat,* 78 N.M. 512, 433 P.2d 229.

(11) Alhough a defendant entered a plea of not guilty, a dismissal thereafter did not constitute an acquittal and further prosecution was not prohibited on the theory of double jeopardy.—*State v. Rhodes,* 76 N.M. 177, 413 P.2d 214.

(12) "Cases are not authority for propositions not considered." —*In re Tartar,* 52 Cal.2d 250, 339 P.2d 553.

ROBBERY

(1) In a robbery prosecution the state is not "bound" by a clerk's testimony that he was not in fear, when there is other evidence to support the conclusion that he acted in fear.—*People v. Renteria,* 39 Cal.Rptr. 213, 393 P.2d 413.

(2) Even though not requested, a trial court must instruct the jury that one of the essential elements of robbery is an intent to steal.—*People v. Ford,* 36 Cal.Rptr. 620 388 P.2d 892.

(3) A codefendant pushed open the doors of a saloon, thrust his head inside and withdrew immediately, then crossed the street, joined the defendant and they got masks and weapons and then they were arrested. The court held that pushing the door open and partially entering was an overt act, enough to constitute an attempt to rob.—*People v. Moran,* 18 Cal.App. 209, 122 Pac. 969.

(4) Defendant asked T. to commit robbery with him. T. acted as a confederate and went into the building while the defendant waited outside. The defendant also supplied T. with a weapon which T. took into building with him. The court held that these acts were enough to sustain a conviction of attempted robbery against both men.—*People v. DuVeau,* 94 N.Y. Supp. 225, 105 App.Div. 381.

(5) The defendant, masked, entered a bank, forced a clerk into the vault, found that he couldn't close the vault and fled. The court held this was an attempted robbery.—*State v. Woodard,* 309 Mo. 19, 273 S.W. 1047.

(6) The defendant and others, intending to rob, entered a gambling room, ordered the people to put their hands up at gun point and then they were interrupted by the police: attempted robbery. —*State v. Waite,* 141 Wash. 429, 251 Pac. 855.

(7) The defendant pointed his gun at the victim and ordered him to hold up his hands: attempted robbery.—*Holbrook v. State,* (Ga.App.), 138 S.E. 919.

(8) In a robbery prosecution it is immaterial whether the gun was loaded or unloaded as long as the victim was put in fear.— *Hayes v. State,* 211 Md. 111, 126 A.2d 576.

(9) The defendant and the victim argued and the defendant and his friends knocked the victim unconscious and then took his money. This is robbery, said the court. The intent to steal may arise after a fight in which the victim is rendered unconscious.—*Turner v. State,* 198 S.W.2d 890.

(10) In a robbery prosecution, the fact that the victim is unconscious when the property is taken from him is immaterial to the charge.—*Mitchell v. State,* 408 P.2d 566.

(11) When a robbery occurs during a kidnapping, the crime becomes "kidnapping for robbery" from the beginning whether or not the kidnapper originally intended to rob the victim.—*In re Ward,* 51 Cal.Rptr. 272, 414 P.2d 400.

(12) Where the kidnapping occurs after the robbery it is still "kidnapping for robbery" if there is a reasonable inference that the victim was transported to effect the escape of the robber or to take the victim to some place where he could not easily sound an alarm.—*People v. Martin,* 58 Cal.Rptr. 481, 250 Cal.App.2d 263.

SEARCH AND SEIZURE

(1) Not all evidence is inadmissible because it would not have come to light but for the illegal actions of the police.—*Swinney v. United States,* 391 F.2d 190.

(2) Circumstances authorizing the police to make a temporary detention may be short of that required for probable cause to make an arrest.—*People v. Davis,* 67 Cal.Rptr. 54, 260 Cal.App.2d 186.

(3) A citizen who says he is the victim of a crime or a witness to a crime is a "reliable informant" even though his reliability has not been proven or tested before.—*People v. Waller,* 67 Cal.-Rptr. 8, 260 Cal.App.2d 131.

(4) The test of whether the admission of illegally seized evidence is harmless error is whether that evidence might have contributed to the conviction. If it might have, it is not harmless.—*Rosenthall v. Henderson,* 389 F.2d 514.

(5) A failure to advise a defendant that he had a right to deny consent to search is a factor in determining whether the consent was voluntary.—*Rosenthall v. Henderson,* 389 F.2d 514.

(6) Where the police had permission from one person to go to the bedroom which he shared with the defendant and open a blue bag that was in the bedroom, bloody clothing of the defendant's found in the bag was admissible because the police did not know that that bag did not belong to the person who gave them permission.—*Gladden v. Frazier,* 388 F.2d 777.

(7) The Fourth Amendment applies to government premises.—*United States v. Hagarty,* 388 F.2d 713.

(8) An officer need not give the *Miranda* warning before receiving a valid consent to search.—*State v. Oldham,* 438 P.2d 275.

(9) A defendant may not complain of a warrantless search and seizure of his father's car.—*Petition of Gallagher,* 150 Mont. 476, 436 P.2d 530.

(10) The prohibition against the admission of any evidence seized in violation of the Fourth Amendment does not apply to such seizures by private persons not acting under direction of police.—*People v. Katzman,* 66 Cal.Rptr. 319, 258 Cal.App.2d 777.

(11) Viewing the inside of the defendant's garage through cracks in the partition from an adjoining garage and observing stolen articles in the garage leased by the defendant is not a "search."—*People v. Lees,* 64 Cal.Rptr. 888, 257 Cal.App.2d 363.

(12) A statute requiring vehicles to stop for a mechanical and equipment check is not unconstitutional.—*People v. De La Torre,* 64 Cal.Rptr. 804, 257 Cal.App.2d 162.

(13) A "consent to search" is not ipso facto involuntary because given while the defendant was in custody.—*McNear v. Rhay,* 65 Wash.2d 530, 398 P.2d 732.

(14) The Fourth Amendment guarantees do not apply to things seized by Mexican officers in Mexico (not under the direction of United States police) and such evidence is admissible in a United States court (apparently even though seized by Mexican police under what the United States would call unlawful conditions).—*Brulay v. United States,* 383 F.2d 345; *Robson v. United States,* 279 F.Supp. 631.

(15) A jail is not a constitutionally protected place within the Fourth Amendment and a conversation between the defendant and a friend may be overheard, transcribed and introduced into evidence.—*Lanza v. New York*, 370 U.S. 139, 8 L.Ed.2d 384, 82 S.Ct. 1218.

(16) Property found on the person of the defendant in a search incident to an illegal arrest is not admissible.—*Green v. United States*, 386 F.2d 953.

(17) When officers entered a house to deal with what they thought was an emergency and saw hypodermic needles and marijuana in an open coffee can, they could properly seize them without a search warrant.—*People v. Kampmann*, 65 Cal.Rptr. 798, 258 A.C.A. 629.

(18) The granting of a motion to suppress is not appealable.—*Ballard v. Superior Court, San Diego County*, 44 Cal.Rptr. 291.

(19) Where an officer lawfully is somewhere where he sees contraband in plain sight, not only may he seize this contraband but it is his duty to do so.—*People v. Kampmann*, 65 Cal.Rptr. 798, 258 A.C.A. 629.

(20) An officer who is pursuing a suspected robber in hot pursuit need not stop and get a search warrant for the vehicle and evidence once the robber goes onto private property (to which he is also a sranger).—*State v. Roberts*, 437 P.2d 731.

(21) The car in which the female was raped is an "instrumentality" of the crime and may be seized and held as evidence.—*State v. McCoy*, 437 P.2d 734.

(22) Consent to a search is not a "confession."—*Heflia v. State*, 161 Tex.Cr. 41, 274 S.W.2d 681.

(23) The fact that physical or other evidence is taken from one in violation of his constitutional rights will not preclude its admission at the trial of another.—*People v. Varnum*, 59 Cal.Rptr. 108, 427 P.2d 772.

(24) The personal effects of an arrestee may be removed and examined to see if they are stolen. They may be returned to him upon his release or preserved for use as evidence at trial.—*People v. Ross,* 60 Cal.Rptr. 254, 429 P.2d 606.

(25) An examination of the defendant's hands under ultraviolet light to determine if he had touched bags which had been dusted with fluorescein powder, was not a search within the Fourth Amendment and did not violate his rights under the Fifth or Sixth either.—*United States v. Richardson,* 388 F.2d 842.

(26) There is no "interception" of a communication if one party to the telephone conversation voluntarily consents to it being monitored.—See *Dryden v. United States,* 391 F.2d 214.

(27) "Probable cause" for a search may rest upon evidence which would not be competent at a trial.—*State v. Kasabucki,* 52 N.J. 110, 244 A.2d 101.

(28) Motions in limine (which are really pretrial motions to suppress) are discussed in 94 *A.L.R.2d* 1082.

(29) It was not a search where the officer merely looked through the window of a station wagon, saw a television set and wrote down the number of the set.—*Chadwick v. State,* 358 Mo. 91, 429 S.W.2d 135.

(30) Fourth Amendment rights do not extend to the grounds around a property (outside the curtilage) even though the officer is a trespasser.—*Cobb v. State,* 213 S.2d 492.

(31) Search of a defendant at the time of booking at the police station is not unreasonable.—*State v. Enstminger,* 160 N.W.2d 480.

(32) A search warrant for a room could not be used to search a person who happened to be in the room at the time of the search.—*State v. Bradbury,* 109 N.H. 105, 243 A.2d 302.

(33) The affidavit for a search warrant may be supplemented by the magistrate's personal interrogation of the affiant.—*State v. Campbell,* 161 N.W.2d 47.

(34) A good discussion of the famous *Wong Sun* case is found in *State v. Traub,* 151 Conn. 246, 196 A.2d 755.

(35) The "fruit of the poisonous tree" doctrine does not require the exclusion of all evidence simply because it would not have come to light except for the illegal action. The test is whether the evidence was obtained by exploitation of the initial illegal action or by means sufficiently distinguishable to be purged of the taint of the illegality.—*Walton v. State,* 245 Ark. 91, 431 S.W.2d 462.

(36) To "dissipate" the *Wong Sun* "taint," you need an intervening independent act by the defendant or a third party which breaks the causal chain connecting the illegality.—*People v. Sesslin,* 67 Cal.Rptr. 409, 439 P.2d 321.

(37) The removal of a particle of fabric from the exterior of the fender of defendant's car parked outside the courthouse was not in violation of the Fourth Amendment.—*Smith v. Commonwealth,* 424 S.W.2d 835.

(38) In an emergency situation, police have the right to enter a home even though there is no intent to arrest, search or seize (police learned of a shooting at the defendant's home and entered when the wife opened the door and then inspected the premises). —*Stevens v. State,* 443 P.2d 600.

(39) A wife could properly consent to the taking of two of her husband's (defendant) suits from their trailer.—*United States v. Alloway,* 397 F.2d 105.

(40) A trial judge is not bound by a pretrial denial of a motion to suppress.—*Washington v. United States,* 401 F.2d 915.

(41) The term in his "presence" in a statute authorizing a citizen's arrest includes not only mere physical proximity but an awareness to the citizen's senses.—*People v. Sjosten,* 68 Cal. Rptr. 832, 262 A.C.A. 574.

(42) Officers who had heard a police report of a robbery and a description of the culprit were justified in arresting the defendant who fitted the description and in taking from him an unlicensed pistol even though it was shown later that the robbery report was false.—*Carter v. State,* 244 A.2d 483.

(43) A court need not advise the defendant of his right to the exclusion of illegally seized evidence prior to the proper acceptance of a guilty plea.—*State v. Cooper,* 161 N.W.2d 728.

(44) Police coming upon an auto accident where the contents of the cars were strewn about were not required to obtain a search warrant before making an inventory of the contents of the autos.—*People v. Roth,* 261 A.C.A. 466, 68 Cal. Rptr. 49.

(45) Hearsay may be used in establishing probable cause to search and seize.—*People v. Hale,* 262 A.C.A. 876, 69 Cal. Rptr. 28.

(46) An illegal arrest, search and seizure does not grant one immunity from prosecution.—*People v. Moore,* 72 Cal. Rptr. 800, 446 P.2d 800.

(47) To obtain a valid consent to search it is not necessary that the officers warn the defendant that any evidence obtained by the search might be admitted in evidence against him.—*State v. Frisby,* 245 A.2d 786.

(48) Excluded evidence under the Fourth Amendment may be introduced for impeachment purposes.—*State v. Cannito,* 183 Neb. 575, 162 N.W.2d 260.

(49) It is not a search to shine a light upon the defendant's hands to reveal fluorescence which had been picked up by the defendant because he had handled stolen money bags.—*United States v. Richardson,* 388 F.2d 842.

(50) The use of deception to gain entrance to make an arrest will not invalidate the arrest as long as no unreasonable force is used.—*Mullaney v. State,* 5 Md.App. 248, 246 A.2d 291.

(51) A failure to inform the accused as to why he is being arrested does not invalidate the arrest.—*Wafers v. State,* 444 P.2d 825.

(52) In any probable cause determination the qualifications and function of the person making the arrest are quite relevant and a narcotics officer's actions should by measured against a standard appropriate for narcotics officers under the circumstances.—*State v. Poe,* 445 P.2d 196.

(53) The assessment of the reasonableness of an arresting officer's conduct should take into consideration the responsibility of the police to prevent crime and to apprehend criminals along with the fact that they often must act on a quick appraisal of the data before them.—*People v. Mills,* 98 Ill.App.2d 248, 240 N.E.2d 302.

(54) An arrest is valid although the warrant is not if the arrest was made upon probable cause.—*People v. Chimel,* 67 Cal.Rptr. 421, 439 P.2d 333.

(55) Even though the magistrate dismisses a complaint because he concluded the evidence was illegally seized his decision on the seizure question is not binding and the charge may be refiled.—*People v. Prewitt,* 52 Cal.2d 330, 341 P.2d 1.

SELF-INCRIMINATION

(1) An examination of the defendant's hands under ultraviolet light to determine if he had touched bags which had been dusted with fluorescein powder, was not a search within the Fourth Amendment and did not violate his rights under the Fifth or Sixth either.—*United States v. Richardson,* 388 F.2d 842.

(2) Even though the defendant was not aware of the reason for cutting his hair when he consented to it, it did not violate his right against self-incrimination when it was used for comparison by an expert.—*State v. Williamson,* 78 N.M. 751, 438 P.2d 161.

(3) At trial a defendant may properly be made to don different costumes, stand up, remove his glasses or reveal tattoo marks on his arms.—*State v. Fisher,* 242 Ore. 419, 410 P.2d 216.

(4) An officer's request that the defendant submit to a blood alcohol test was not a violation of the defendant's constitutional rights.—*State v. Walker,* 199 Kan. 508, 430 P.2d 246.

(5) An instruction telling the jury that they could consider the defendant's refusal to take a breathalyzer test was proper.—*People v. Sudduth,* 55 Cal.Rptr. 393, 421 P.2d 401.

(6) A statute requiring a motorist involved in an accident to give his name does not violate the motorist's privilege against self-incrimination.—*People v. Limon,* 60 Cal.Rptr. 448, 252 Cal. App.2d 575.

(7) Is asking a defendant in the presence of the jury to produce a document a violation of his right against self-incrimination? See 110 *A.L.R.* 101.

(8) The taking of the defendant's fingerprints from the victim's automobile without first advising the defendant of his rights in regard to the prints did not violate his constitutional right against self-incrimination.—*People v. Lewis,* 53 Cal.Rptr. 108, 244 Cal. App.2d 325.

(9) A statute requiring vagrants or loiterers to identify themselves and account for their presence to an officer does not violate that person's right against self-incrimination.—*People v. Weger,* 59 Cal.Rptr. 661, 251 Cal.App.2d 584.

(10) The rule requiring the defendant to explain his possession of recently stolen property or have his failure used against him does not compel him to "take the stand" in violation of the fifth Amendment.—*People v. DeLeon,* 46 Cal.Rptr. 241, 236 Cal.App. 2d 530. See *Pugh v. State,* 416 P.2d 637.

(11) The use of a transmitter and a recording device concealed on a confederate, who had agreed to cooperate in obtaining statements from the defendant did not violate the United States Constitution (4th, 5th or 6th).—*Garrett v. United States,* 382 F.2d 768.

(12) A plea of guilty is not coerced because the defendant was not advised by the court of his right to remain silent when called on to plead.—*Hensley v. State,* 199 Kan. 728, 433 P.2d 344.

(13) A witness before a grand jury may not refuse to testify on the ground that if he commits perjury he would be subject to incrimination.—*State v. Ruggeri,* 19 Utah 2d 216, 429 P.2d 969.

(14) An instruction that if the jury found exculpatory statements of the defendant untrue, they could be considered as evidence of his consciousness of guilt does not violate the Fifth or Sixth Amendments.—*United States v. Smith,* 379 F.2d 628.

(15) The privilege against self-incrimination is waived when a witness has pleaded guilty and been sentenced.—*State v. Nelson,* 246 Ore. 321, 424 P.2d 223.

(16) When a witness invokes his right against self-incrimination, a reversal is justified only when the state consciously and flagrantly tries to build its case out of the inferences arising from the invoking of this privilege.—*United States v. Aiken,* 373 F.2d 294.

(17) Putting a witness on the stand knowing he will take the Fifth is discussed in *State v. Fournier,* 91 N.J.Super. 477, 221 A.2d 225.

(18) Calling the defendant's accomplice to extract from him his claim of privilege against incrimination was reversible error in *De Gesualdo v. People,* 147 Colo. 426, 364 P.2d 374.

(19) Calling the defendant's accomplice after defense counsel has told the court and the state that the accomplice will take the Fifth is ground for reversal.—*State v. Johnson,* 243 Ore. 532, 413 P.2d 383. Apparently contra: *Gonzalez v. People,* 438 P.2d 686.

(20) Where a defendant is charged with murder and is committed to the state asylum before trial, it is not violative of the defendant's right against self-incrimination to have a doctor from the state asylum testify as to the defendant's sanity.—*Hunt v. State,* 248 Ala. 217, 27 S.2d 186.

(21) A compulsory mental examination of a defendant does not violate his privilege against self-incrimination.—*Holt v. United States,* 218 U.S. 245, 54 L.Ed. 1021, 31 S.Ct. 2; Wigmore, 3rd ed. § 2263, § 2265; 28 *J.Crim. C. & Crim.* 261; 59 Har.L.R. 481, 521-523, 25 *A.L.R.2d* 1407; *United States v. Hohn,* 198 F.2d 934; *State v. Nelson,* 162 Ore. 430, 92 P.2d 182.

(22) The examination of a defendant by psychiatrists for the prosecuting attorney without the defendant's counsel being present (or any notice being given to him) does not violate the constitutional rights of the defendant.—*Blocker v. State,* 92 Fla. 878, 110 So. 547. Also *Walters v. State,* 22 Ala.App. 644, 119 So. 248 (where court ordered it done); *State v. Myers,* 220 S.C. 309, 67 S.E.2d 506.

(23) Where a court orders the defendant to be examined at the state's request, the defendant does not become a witness against himself when the doctor testifies.—*State v. Petty,* 32 Nev. 384, 108 Pac. 934. Also *People v. Bundy,* 168 Cal. 777, 145 Pac. 537.

(24) Where a psychiatrist interviewed the defendant at the request of the state, the psychiatrist was an agent of the state with no more right than any such agent to elicit admissions from the defendant without his being informed of his rights, and his admissions of guilt to the psychiatrist should have been excluded. —*People v. Polk,* 44 Cal.Rptr. 773, 402 P.2d 845.

(25) Statements by the accused during a mental examination ordered by the court are admissible in evidence at trial on guilt.—*United States v. Albright*, 388 F.2d 719.

(26) Voice identification is admissible evidence and the defendant may be made to repeat certain words so that the identification may be made without violating his right against self-incrimination.—*State v. Ramirez*, 76 N.M. 72, 412 P.2d 246.

(27) Requiring a defendant to speak so that his voice may be identified is discussed in 16 *A.L.R.2d* 1322.

(28) The state is permitted to take the fingerprints of the defendant in the courtroom during trial.—*United States v. Rundle*, 384 F.2d 997.

(29) Although a defendant need not answer a policeman's questions, there is no prohibition against asking a defendant who has taken the stand as a witness about such silence.—*State v. Zappia*, 8 Ariz.App. 549, 448 P.2d 119.

(30) A urine specimen is admissible although not taken under medical supervision.—*Davis v. District of Columbia*, 247 A.2d 417.

(31) It is consonant with good morals and the Constitution to exploit a criminal's ignorance or stupidity in the detectional process.—*State v. McKnight*, 52 N.J. 35, 243 A.2d 240.

(32) Plainclothes policemen were not required to warn the defendant of her constitutional rights before she smoked a marijuana cigarette in their presence.—*People v. Marinow*, 67 Cal. Rptr. 452, 260 Cal.App.2d 735.

(33) The statement, "You don't have to advise me of my rights, I know more about them than you. I have been picked up and advised many times before," indicates a valid waiver of the *Miranda* rights.—*State v. Perez*, 182 Neb. 701, 157 N.W.2d 165.

(34) "It should be made clear that once Miranda's mandate was complied with at the threshold of the questioning it was not necessary to repeat the warnings at the beginning of each successive interview. To adopt an automatic second-warning system would be to add a perfunctory ritual to police procedures rather than providing the meaningful set of procedural safeguards envisioned by *Miranda*."—*People v. Hill,* 39 Ill.2d 125, 233 N.E.2d 367.

(35) Although the defendant confessed the killing of his wife to a friend at a bar and the friend called a sheriff and the defendant then told the sheriff the same thing, the accusatory stage was not reached until the physical facts indicating that crime had been disclosed (discovery of the body back at the defendant's house).—*State v. Zachmeier,* 441 P.2d 737.

(36) Under *Miranda,* officers need not warn a person able to afford an attorney that if he is not able to hire an attorney one will be afforded to him.—*State v. Devoe,* 430 S.W.2d 164.

(37) *Massiah* does not apply where, after indictment and appointment of counsel, a third person, without aid from or knowledge of the police, obtains admissions from the accused and then relates them to the police.—*People v. Milani,* 39 Ill.2d 22, 233 N.E.2d 398.

(38) The defendant was not in a *Miranda*-type custody when officers appeared outside his locked front screen door and asked his name, whether he was an exconvict and whether he possessed a forbidden weapon.—*People v. Merchant,* 67 Cal.Rptr. 459, 260 Cal.App.2d 875.

(39) Officers are not required to repeat the *Miranda* warnings every time their interrogation touches upon a separate crime.—*State v. Jennings,* 104 Ariz. 6, 448 P.2d 62.

(40) Sobriety tests (writing name, picking up coins, touching hand to nose) and motion pictures of the defendant are not in violation of his self-incrimination privilege.—*City of Piqua v. Hinger,* 15 Ohio St.2d 110, 238 N.E.2d 766.

(41) The defendant's self-incrimination privilege is not violated by taking his fingerprints without affording him counsel or warning him of his self-incrimination privilege.—*Washington v. State*, 434 S.W.2d 138.

(42) A physician, suspecting his patient of nothing criminal, is not required to give the patient the *Miranda* warnings before, during or after the examination.—*Edwards v. State*, 244 Ark. 1145, 429 S.W.2d 92.

(43) Any words which convey the substance of the *Miranda* warnings are sufficient.—*United States v. Vanterpool*, 394 F.2d 697.

SENTENCE

(1) The imposing of a sentence is not an element of the "conviction."—*State v. Silva*, 78 N.M. 286, 430 P.2d 783.

(2) Where the defendant was given probation on condition he spend the first ten months in the county jail, the condition did not render the crime a misdemeanor.—*People v. Esparza*, 61 Cal. Rptr. 167, 253 Cal.App.2d 362.

(3) A prisoner's sentence is tolled by his escape and it does not begin to run again until his return.—*Phillips v. Dutton*, 378 F.2d 898.

(4) It is not within the power of a trial court to give credit for time served unless a statute specifically authorizes it.—*William v. Page*, 430 P.2d 345.

(5) A court cannot preclude the possibility of parole unless the statute authorizes it.—*Spillers v. State*, 436 P.2d 18.

(6) The Fifth Amendment does not prohibit a different punishment on a retrial.—*United States v. White*, 382 F.2d 445.

(7) An increased sentence on retrial or a denial of credit for that part of invalid sentence already served is a violation of the double jeopardy clause.—*Patton v. State of North Carolina,* 381 F.2d 636.

(8) The defendant was not put twice in jeopardy when the prosecution used his 1960 conviction to increase the penalty on his current conviction.—*Anderson v. Wilson,* 397 F.2d 255.

(9) Codefendants may be punished differently for the same crime and the fact that one gets probation and the other does not, does not constitute cruel and unusual punishment.—*Bates v. State,* 436 P.2d 27.

(10) "Plea bargaining" in which the defendant entered a plea of guilty to a forgery charge in exchange for the state's not filing similar charges and a habitual criminal charge did not constitute coercion which would require vacating and setting aside the sentence.—*Smith v. People,* 428 P.2d 69.

(11) There is nothing unconstitutional in sentencing a youthful offender (juvenile) under the Federal Youth Corrections Act to a period of incarceration longer than he could have received if he had been sentenced as an adult.—*Harvin v. United States,* 245 A.2d 307.

(12) The mere offer to recommend a reduced sentence does not constitute duress when speaking of guilty pleas.—*People v. Bowman,* 40 Ill.2d 116, 239 N.E.2d 433.

(13) Upon a guilty plea an involuntary confession is not admissible in a hearing to determine degree of guilt.—*United States ex rel. Sanders v. Maroney,* 397 F.2d 267.

(14) The fact that the prosecuting authorities utilized the Habitual Offender statute only when the prior conviction was within their state did not give rise to a denial of equal protection. —*State v. Baldonado,* 79 N.M. 175, 441 P.2d 215.

SUPPRESSION

(1) The state is not required to call any particular witness or make any particular test. In an assault case (with a gun), the fact that they did not test the gun for fingerprints or take photos of the bullet holes in the door does not establish any intentional suppression of evidence requiring a reversal.—*People v. Wright,* 66 Cal.Rptr. 95, 258 Cal.App.2d 762.

(2) The state is not required to report to the defendant all they learn about the case and the witnesses (WOW!).—*In re Imbler,* 387 P.2d 6, 35 Cal.Rptr. 293.

(3) Although the state did not introduce the results of a police fingerprint test in a burglary case, this was no suppression since all of the elements were present without the can (allegedly used to break into the store) and thus the trial court properly refused to instruct in the suppression of evidence.—*People v. Mestas,* 61 Cal.Rptr. 731, 253 Cal.App.2d 780.

(4) The state's failure to call a witness is not a suppression of evidence.—*Boucher v. Warden,* 5 Md.App. 51, 245 A.2d 420.

TELEPHONES

(1) There is no "interception" of a communication if one party to the telephone conversation voluntarily consents to it being monitored.—See *Dryden v. United States,* 391 F.2d 214.

(2) Identification of a voice on the telephone may be proved circumstantially.—*Grogan v. United States,* 386 F.2d 300.

(3) Telephone service is a "valuable thing" within a false pretenses (theft) statute.—*Stokes v. State,* 366 P.2d 425.

(4) Testimony that a telephone conversation took place is not objectionable as hearsay.—*People v. Gonzales,* 87 Cal.Rptr. 551, 439 P.2d 655.

THEFT

(1) When it was shown that the suits found in the defendant's possession were unaltered, of different sizes, bore numbers and tags customarily used by the victim store, were not sold by any of that store's regularly assigned personnel and were not the subject of a recorded sale or authorized removal from the store, the jury could conclude that they were unlawfully appropriated from the store.—*State v. Meyers,* 65 Wash.2d 911, 400 P.2d 372.

(2) An escapee's pushing an automobile down a road to a point where it had not even left the owner's premises was not a "taking" in the ordinary understanding of that term.—*Marin v. Comm. of Va.,* 365 F.2d 549.

(3) It is immaterial in a prosecution for theft from the person that the "person" cannot testify to an observation of the actual theft (an officer saw it).—*People v. De La Paz,* 46 Cal.Rptr. 614, 237 Cal.App.2d 81.

(4) Even though a bank held title to the car, it was not necessary to prove a lack of consent from both before a conviction for stealing the car would be sustained (equitable owner's testimony was enough).—*Raullerson v. People,* 159 Colo. 395, 412 P.2d 236.

(5) Telephone service is a "valuable thing" within a false pretense (theft) statute.—*Stokes v. State,* 366 P.2d 425.

(6) It is not necessary to account for all of the missing stolen property or even to show it to be in the accused's possession.—*State v. Weinstein,* 244 N.C. 645, 31 S.E.2d 920, 156 *A.L.R.* 625.

(7) A repaired torn check may be the subject of a charge of larceny and forgery (against a defense of "spoilation" rendering it non-negotiable.)—*State v. Romero,* 146 Mont. 77, 404 P.2d 500.

(8) The nonconsent of the owner to the taking of the property may be shown by circumstantial evidence. Here the owner never testified but the caretaker of the property (house or building from which property taken) did. The court said this plus circumsances of taking were enough (plus the fact that the owner's absence was satisfactorily explained).—*Kearson v. State,* 166 So. 832.

(9) Non-negotiable instruments may be the subjects of larceny by check.—*Faulkner v. State,* 445 P.2d 815.

(10) Judicial notice may be taken of the fact that property has "some" value.—*People v. Tassone,* 41 Ill.2d 7, 241 N.E.2d 419.

TILL-TAPPING

(1) Till-tapping expertise is discussed in 100 *A.L.R.2d* 1433.

TRIAL (SPEEDY)

(1) An arrest five and one-half months after the state knew the defendant had committed the crime is not unreasonable. Here the delay was necessary to keep the officer's identity secret while he was continuing with other investigations.—*People v. Alvarado,* 66 Cal.Rptr. 41.

(2) A ten-year delay in bringing the defendant to trial on a murder charge was not, by itself, too long to result in the deprivation of the defendant's constitutional rights.—*State v. Alter,* 67 Wash.2d 111, 406 P.2d 765.

(3) The constitutional guaranty of a speedy trial has no reference to a preliminary examination.—*Cooper v. State,* 196 Kan. 421, 411 P.2d 652.

(4) It is too late to move for a dismissal on the ground that the state has failed to bring the case on for trial within 60 days, after the trial begins or is just about to begin (like on the morning of trial).—*State v. Keller,* 65 Wash.2d 907, 400 P.2d 370.

(5) The defendant's right to a speedy trial is waived only by affirmative action on his part (like express consent to a delay or a request for one); never by inaction of the defendant.—*Hicks v. People,* 148 Colo. 26, 364 P.2d 877.

(6) If a defendant desires a speedy trial, he should move for it by way of a habeas corpus ad prosequendum.—*Gunter v. Okla. County Dist. Ct.,* 434 P.2d 493.

(7) A defendant's consent (and waiver of his right to a speedy trial) will be presumed where he does not object to a delay past the time period set for speedy trials.—*People v. Chaney,* 43 Cal. Rptr. 280; *People v. McGill,* 65 Cal.Rptr. 482, 257 A.C.A. 859.

(8) A delay to determine the defendant's mental capacity to stand trial is "good cause" for continuing the trial past the 60-day limit.—*People v. McGill,* 65 Cal.Rptr. 482, 257 A.C.A. 859.

(9) The fact that a codefendant has a prior criminal record does not require the granting of separate trials.—*Alford v. Commonwealth,* 432 S.W.2d 414.

TRUTH SERUM

(1) You cannot rehabilitate a witness with a doctor who put her under truth serum and will testify that the witness told him the truth.—*Knight v. State,* 97 S.2d 115.

VALUE

(1) An owner may testify to the value of his property.—*Ingersol v. Seattle-First Nat. Bank*, 63 Wash.2d 354, 387 P.2d 538.

(2) The purchase price of an article; its condition at that time; and its saleable value at a secondhand store are elements for a jury to consider in determining the value of an article.—*Lefthand v. State*, 398 P.2d 98.

(3) Judicial notice may be taken of the fact that property has "some" value.—*People v. Tassone*, 41 Ill.2d 7, 241 N.E.2d 419.

(4) Where there was an issue as to the amount of money stolen it was not in violation of the Best Evidence Rule to permit oral testimony by the victim as to how much was taken although he also testified that he had made calculations on an adding machine.—*State v. Swanson*, 440 P.2d 492.

VARIANCE

(1) A variance is "material" if it might mislead the defense or expose the defendant to being twice put in jeopardy.—*Mitchell v. State*, 408 P.2d 566.

(2) The variance between an information showing the ownership of property in a certain named store and proof that the owner of the property was really the owner of the store (the store had the same name as its owner) is immaterial.—*Smith v. State*, 378 P.2d 790.

VENUE

(1) Publicity concerning a statewide "soft on crime" controversy and stories about other notorious criminal cases (which had nothing to do with the defendant's case) did not entitle him to a change of venue.—*Mears v. State,* 422 P.2d 230.

(2) "We do not think the court erred in over-ruling the motion for change of venue, based, as it was on the affidavits of defendant's attorneys. The court held that they were not disinterested persons, and so do we."—*Territory v. Vialpando,* 8 N.M. 211, 42 Pac. 64.

(3) Evidence that the stabbing occurred on Second Avenue in Seattle is sufficient to establish venue in King County, Washington.—*State v. Rogers,* 66 Wash.2d 358, 402 P.2d 501.

(4) A good discussion on the general law concerning a change of venue appears in *State v. Taborsky,* 20 Conn.Sup. 242, 131 A.2d 337, 60 Col. L.Rev. 349.

(5) Venue need be proved only by a preponderance of the evidence to support a conviction.—*State v. Glasscock,* 76 N.M. 367, 415 P.2d 56.

(6) A citizen of the United States may be punished in the United States for conspiring to smuggle amphetamine tablets into the United States even though the acts leading to the crime were committed in Mexico.—*Brulay v. United States,* 383 F.2d 345.

(7) Venue may be proved by circumstantial evidence.—*Holsenbake v. State,* 416 P.2d 178.

(8) Testimony that the house where the killing occurred was in Ware County was not a "mere conclusion" and was admissible. —*Holmes v. State,* 224 Ga.App. 553, 163 S.E.2d 803.

VIEW

(1) There was no error in refusing to allow the jury a view of the premises in a prosecution for rape.—*Spillers v. State,* 436 P.2d 18. (I'll bet that was a relief to somebody!)

(2) A jury view is not evidence. It assists the jury in comprehending the evidence.—*Spillers v. State,* 436 P.2d 18.

VOICE

(1) Voice identification is admissible evidence and the defendant may be made to repeat certain words so that the identification may be made without violating his right against self-incrimination.—*State v. Ramirez,* 76 N.M. 72, 412 P.2d 246.

(2) Requiring a defendant to speak so that his voice may be identified is discussed in 16 *A.L.R.2d* 1322.

(3) Identification of a voice on the telephone may be proved circumstantially.—*Grogan v. United States,* 386 F.2d 300.

WEAPONS

(1) Although a sawed-off shotgun was not ready for use because it was broken down into its three component parts at the time of its discovery, the defendant's possession was still unlawful. —*People v. Guyette,* 41 Cal.Rptr. 875, 231 Cal.App.2d 460.

(2) A tear gas fountain pen capable only of discharging tear gas is not a "loaded pistol."—*State v. Umbrello,* 106 N.H. 336, 211 A.2d 400.

WITNESSES

(1) The state is not bound by the testimony of its own witness as to an excuse for the crime where there is other evidence for the state showing a lack of it.—*People v. Chapman,* 67 Cal.Rptr. 601, 261 Cal.App.2d 149.

(2) A witness may be called in rebuttal who has not been endorsed on the information.—*Dickerson v. State,* 422 P.2d 213.

(3) The testimony of an accomplice is not excludable because he refused to answer questions on a deposition prior to the trial. —*State v. Corliss* (*Mont.*), 150 Mont. 40, 430 P.2d 632.

(4) If a hostile witness testifies that what is in a written statement is true, the statement may be introduced as part of that witness' testimony.—*Stewart v. Baltimore* & *GR Co.,* 137 F.2d 527; *Zimberg v. United States,* 142 F.2d 132; *Jenkins v. 313-321*

W. 37th St. Corp., 284 N.Y. 397, 31 N.E.2d 503; *United States v. Freundlich,* 95 F.2d 376; *Pulitzer v. Chapman,* 337 Mo. 298, 85 S.W.2d 400; *State v. Jolly,* 112 Mont. 352, 116 P.2d 686; *Tripp v. United States,* 295 F.2d 418.

(5) Whether to replay all or part of the testimony for the jury is within the discretion of the trial court.—*Price v. State,* 437 P.2d 330.

(6) After the verdict, it is too late to complain (for the first time) that a witness was not sworn before he testified.—*Brown v. State,* 171 Tex.Cr. 692, 353 S.W.2d 425.

(7) A crime against the child of a spouse is a crime against the spouse.—*Balltrip v. People,* 157 Colo. 108, 401 P.2d 259, 82 *A.L.R.* 644.

(8) Calling the defendant's accomplice after defense counsel has told the court and the state that the accomplice will take the Fifth is ground for a reversal.—*State v. Johnson,* 243 Ore. 532, 413 P.2d 383. Apparently contra: *Gonzalez v. People,* 438 P.2d 686.

(9) A defendant, after he once takes the stand as a witness and after he closes his case, may be recalled for further cross-examination (here to lay a predicate for further testimony).—*Chatman v. State,* 145 S.2d 707.

(10) The admissibility of "prior trial" testimony to cover gaps or omissions due to his failure to remember presently is discussed in 129 *A.L.R.* 843.

(11) The fact that a witness at the trial had not testified at the preliminary examination did not deny the defendant his constitutional right to confront witnesses.—*In re Malloy,* 47 Cal. Rptr. 345, 424 P.2d 929.

(12) On voir dire to determine the competency of a child witness, questions concerning the facts of the crime are immaterial to the question of whether she could remember and truthfully recount.—*People v. McIntyre,* 64 Cal.Rptr. 530, 256 Cal. App.2d 894.

(13) Admission of an absent witness' preliminary examination testimony is valid even though at the preliminary examination the witness had not been fully or adequately cross-examined.—*People v. Berger,* 66 Cal.Rptr. 213, 258 Cal.App.2d 622.

(14) A mistrial is equivalent to a "former trial" under a rule which says a transcript of a "former trial" is admissible where the witness is absent.—*People v. Schwarz,* 248 Pac. 990.

(15) The Uniform Act to Secure the Attendance of Witnesses From Without the State was not intended to limit the use of the prior testimony of an absent witness.—*State v. Lesco,* 194 Kan. 555, 400 P.2d 695.

(16) The test of whether to admit prior testimony is not so much the unavailability of the witness, but the unavailability of his testimony. Here a court reporter was permitted to testify to the questions and answers of the witness at a former trial when the witness refused to say anything other than his name and status as an inmate of the penitentiary at the second trial.—*Johnson v. People,* 153 Colo. 56, 384 P.2d 454.

(17) A witness does not have to give the specific words spoken by a defendant when retelling the conversation with the defendant.—*Lugo v. United States,* 370 F.2d 992.

(18) The privilege against self-incrimination is waived when a witness has pleaded guilty and been sentenced.—*State v. Nelson,* 424 P.2d 223.

(19) When a witness invokes his right against self-incrimination, a reversal is justified only when the state consciously and flagrantly tries to build its case out of the inferences arising from the invoking of this privilege.—*United States v. Aiken,* 373 F.2d 294.

(20) Putting a witness on the stand knowing he will take the Fifth is discussed in *State v. Fournier,* 91 N.J.Super. 477, 221 A.2d 225.

(21) Calling the defendant's accomplice to extract from him his claim of privilege against incrimination was reversible error in *De Gesualdo v. People,* 147 Colo. 426, 364 P.2d 374.

(22) The use of the defendant's parole officer as a witness against him was not an allusion to his prior record.—*People v. Saldivar,* 57 Cal.Rptr. 731, 249 Cal.App.2d 670.

(23) Where a codefendant had entered a guilty plea, the state could "lawfully expect" him to testify in conformity with his confession. Thus the state did not commit error in telling the jury that they expected the codefendant to testify.—*State v. Frazier,* 418 P.2d 841.

(24) It is prejudicial to require the defense to request, receive and read *Jencks*-type "statements" in front of the jury.—*Gregory v. United States,* 369 F.2d 185.

(25) The fact that the witness is a convicted perjurer concerns only the credibility not the competency of his testimony.—*State v. Barick,* 143 Mont. 273, 389 P.2d 170.

(26) A witness' capacity to perceive or remember is for the jury to consider in weighing his credibility but that capacity is not a basis for excluding his testimony.—*State v. Poulos,* 196 Kan. 253, 411 P.2d 694.

(27) The foundation required for showing the bias or prejudice of a witness is discussed in 87 *A.L.R.2d* 407.

(28) A witness before a grand jury may not refuse to testify on the ground that if he commits perjury he would be subject to incrimination.—*State v. Ruggeri,* 19 Utah 2d 216, 429 P.2d 969.

(29) "The County Attorney, if he knows any facts, may, like any other witness, be sworn and submit himself to examination and cross-examination. . . "—*Hash v. State,* 48 Ariz. 43, 59 P.2d 305.

(30) Calling the prosecutor as a witness is discussed in 149 *A.L.R.* 1305.

(31) The state may call defense counsel as a witness subject to the discretion of the court but before defense counsel testifies the court should hold a hearing to determine if such evidence is material and admissible and if it is, other counsel should be provided for the defendant.—*Marlow v. State,* 432 P.2d 999.

(32) "Where a witness uses any paper to refresh his memory while he is on the witness stand, the opposing side, on proper demand, may examine the paper and use it on cross-examination."—*Jackson v. United States,* 250 F.2d 897.

(33) A discussion of refreshing the recollection of a witness by memos or other writings appears in 125 *A.L.R.* 19.

(34) The defendant could not claim prejudice because a witness against him had been granted immunity from any crime growing out of transactions about which he was being questioned.—*State v. Dickens,* 66 Wash.2d 58, 401 P.2d 321.

(35) A defendant has no constitutional question to raise because the state would not grant one of his witnesses immunity so that the witness could testify for the defendant.—*Morrison v. United States,* 365 F.2d 521.

(36) The state is not required to call every witness even though they are subpoenaed.—*State v. Love,* 77 Ariz. 46, 266 P.2d 1079.

(37) The rule that an inference may be drawn against a party for failure to call a witness that that witness' testimony would be unfavorable to the party does not apply to the government when it is granted the privilege of nondisclosure—such as with an informer.—*United States v. Jackson,* 384 F.2d 825.

(38) Where there are no facilities for separating or sequestering witnesses, it is not error not to do so.—*State v. Woods,* 191 Kan. 433, 381 P.2d 533.

(39) The court may, when asked to sequester witnesses, permit an officer witness to remain with the prosecutor.—*Dickens v. State,* 398 P.2d 1008.

(40) When the defendant invokes the rule of sequestration of witnesses, if he elects to testify in his own behalf, he must precede all other witnesses for the defense.—*Spaulding v. United States,* 279 F.2d 65.

(41) The state's prospective witnesses are under no duty to disclose to the defendant's counsel what their testimony will be. —*Corbett v. People,* 153 Colo. 457, 387 P.2d 409.

(42) Because a witness refused to discuss his testimony with defense counsel is no reason to exclude his testimony.—*People v. Spinuzzi,* 149 Colo. 391, 369 P.2d 427.

(43) A defendant who objects to his "wife" testifying against him has the burden of proving that the witness is married to him. —*State v. Clyde,* 47 Hawaii 345, 388 P.2d 846.

(44) In the prosecution of a husband for attempted murder, a wife's claim to the physician-patient privilege was properly overruled as to information gained by physicians who treated her after her husband tried to kill her because the evidence would cause little additional embarrassment and would not subject her to any criminal liability.—*State v. Boehme,* 71 Wash.2d 621, 430 P.2d 527.

(45) "Plea bargaining" with codefendants who testified against the defendant did not, ipso facto, constitute coerced testimony against the defendant.—*Minkin v. United States,* 383 F.2d 427.

(46) Statements of a third person in answer to inquiries about an absent witness and the inquiries themselves are admissible to prove that a diligent search for the witness was made.—*People v. Thomas,* 164 Cal.App.2d 571, 331 P.2d 82.

(47) The degree of positiveness in identification goes to the weight of such testimony and not the admissibility.—*People v. Gonzales,* 67 Cal.Rptr. 551, 439 P.2d 655.

(48) An owner may testify to the value of his property.—*Ingersol v. Seattle-First Nat. Bank,* 63 Wash.2d 354, 387 P.2d 538.

(49) An officer may testify to conversations he heard over a receiver concealed on an informer's person.—*United States v. Jackson,* 390 F.2d 317; *Handsferd v. United States,* 390 F.2d 373.

(50) A jury need not be instructed that the uncorroborated testimony of a police narcotics officer must be viewed with suspicion and acted on with caution, or that such a rule is applicable to new recruits or novice officers.—*Bush v. United States,* 375 F.2d 602.

(51) A person may be legally and properly identified by his size, height, movements, features, mannerisms and clothing.—*State v. Williamson,* 78 N.M. 751, 438 P.2d 161.

(52) It is proper for the state to ask the psychiatrist if he was appointed by the court to examine the defendant.—*Hunt v. State,* 248 Ala. 217, 27 So.2d 180. Also *Comm'n v. Musto,* 348 Pa. 300, 35 A.2d 307 (not really a court order here, just consent by court to state's attorney to have it done before trial).

(53) The testimony of a doctor is admissible where the doctor is not consulted for treatment.—107 *A.L.R.* 1495.

(54) In a sex case it may be permissible to introduce psychiatric testimony concerning the mental and emotional condition of the "victim."—*Ballard v. Superior Court of San Diego County,* 49 Cal.Rptr. 302, 410 P.2d 838.

(55) You cannot rehabilitate a witness with a doctor who put her under truth serum and will testify that the witness told the truth.—*Knight v. State,* 97 S.2d 115.

(56) Evidence of prior inconsistent statements to impeach the defendant may be considered not only for the purpose of testing the defendant's credibility but with all other evidence in determining his guilt.—*People v. Underwood,* 37 Cal.Rptr. 313, 389 P.2d 937.

(57) The impeachment of a witness by medical testimony that the witness is a liar is discussed in 15 *A.L.R.* 932.

(58) Even though the defendant is permitted to testify at trial on the limited issue of the voluntariness of his confession, he may be impeached by prior felony convictions.—*Boone v. State,* 2 Md. App. 80, 233 A.2d 476.

(59) Permitting witnesses to point to the defendant in open court is not error.—*State v. Dunn,* 91 Idaho 870, 434 P.2d 88.

(60) The fact that at trial the state does not call all the witnesses upon whose testimony the indictment was based does not violate the defendant's constitutional right of confrontation.—*Couser v. State,* 4 Md.App. 543, 243 A.2d 639.

(61) The defendant has no constitutional right to require that the Uniform Act to Secure the Attendance of Witnesses From Without the State be used to obtain the attendance of out of state witnesses.—*People v. Cavanaugh,* 70 Cal.Rptr. 438, 444 P.2d 110.

(62) A witness' violation of the witness-exclusion rule does not disqualify him as a witness but may be considered as to his credibility.—*Pippins v. State,* 224 Ga. 462, 162 S.E.2d 338.

(63) A witness' testimony is not automatically suspect because he is a homosexual.—*People v. Rowland,* 69 Cal.Rptr. 269, 262 A.C.A. 886.

(64) The state's failure to call a witness is not a suppression of evidence.—*Boucher v. Warden,* 5 Md.App. 51, 245 A.2d 420.

(65) There is a fairly good discussion of the competency and reliability of narcotics addicts as witnesses in *State v. Booth,* 423 S.W.2d 820.

(66) Homosexuality or an unnatural relationship is admissible if and when it shows the bias, interest or motive of a witness.—*People v. Rowland,* 69 Cal.Rptr. 269, 262 A.C.A. 886.

(67) There is no right on the part of the defendant to have minor witnesses questioned as to their competency outside the presence of the jury.—*Ramer v. State,* 40 Wis.2d 79, 161 N.W.2d 209.

(68) Allowing witnesses to be impeached by their prior inconsistent statements does not deprive the defendant of any constitutional rights.—*Gaitan v. People,* 447 P.2d 1001.

(69) Although a defendant need not answer a policeman's questions, there is no prohibition against asking a defendant who has taken the stand as a witness about such silence.—*State v. Zappia,* 8 Ariz.App. 549, 448 P.2d 119.

(70) Permitting a prosecution psychiatrist to sit in the courtroom and listen to the defense psychiatrist and then testify on rebuttal even though the "witness rule" (exclusion) had been invoked is not error.—*Wallace v. State,* 447 P.2d 30.

(71) The fact that a witness failed to identify another person involved in the robbery has no bearing or materiality on the witness' identification of the defendant.—*State v. Hunsucker,* 3 N.C. App. 281, 164 S.E.2d 507.

(72) The prosecution is not required to inform the defendant, prior to trial, of the criminal record of the state's witnesses.—*Hemphill v. United States,* 392 F.2d 45.

(73) Showing a photograph of the defendant to a witness before his in-court identification is not in violation of the constitution where there is no evidence that the picture was used to prime the witness or to bolster an otherwise shaky identification.—*People v. Smith,* 66 Cal.Rptr. 551, 259 Cal.App.2d 814.

(74) A victim's declarations are not inadmissible at trial even though the victim himself was ruled incompetent as a witness.—*State v. Simmons,* 52 N.J. 538, 247 A.2d 313.